DREAMWRECKS
OF THE CARIBBEAN

Diving the best shipwrecks of the region

CATHY SALISBURY & DOMINIQUE SERAFINI

Text by Cathy Salisbury and Dominique Serafini
Illustrations and paintings by Dominique Serafini
Photography and design by Cathy Salisbury

Published by Love of the Sea Publishing

DreamWrecks of the Caribbean - Diving the best shipwrecks of the region
ISBN#: 978-0-973059-83-0 (paperback)

www.dreamwrecks.com

Cathy Salisbury cathsalis@gmail.com
Dominique Serafini domiserafini@gmail.com

Cover: The wreck of Our Confidence, Bonaire - digital painting by Cathy Salisbury
Back cover: The shipwrecks of the Bay of Saint-Pierre, Martinique by Dominique Serafini
Page 3: The wreck of the Willaurie, New Providence, Bahamas
Page 5: The wreck of the Windjammer, Bonaire, BES Islands

LOVE OF THE SEA
PUBLISHING

Dominique Serafini and Cathy Salisbury

>>INTRODUCTION

TREASURES OF THE CARIBBEAN

Gold and silver bars, coins, precious jewels, bronze statues, Greek amphora, Chinese porcelain... These treasures, hidden in the heart of sunken shipwrecks, capture the imagination of people the world over. They are what dreams are made of.

**The Galleon Fleet, Las Aves, Venezuela.
Opposite Page: USS LST-467, St Thomas, USVIs**

The thought of finding sunken treasure is a global fascination, making professional divers and non-swimmers alike dream of pirate loot, gold doubloons and sparkling diamonds. However, most shipwrecks have no precious cargo or treasure chests waiting to be found. Most are just empty carcasses. But even if they have no great riches to be discovered, these wrecks still have tremendous value. An anchor lying on a bed of sand, old cannons, broken pieces of pottery, iron scraps—all are signs of a past life and a rich history to be discovered and cherished.

Over the years, the forces of the sea destroy these wrecks: the waves and currents break their wooden structures into pieces and erode their metallic parts. Along the seabed, the ocean spits out the remains of the vessels it has swallowed and digested. All that remains of these glorious ships are the odd pieces, that serve as clues to the vessels' past.

It isn't only the sea that damages wrecks—often man also helps in the destruction process. With the use of dynamite, welding guns, hooks, chains and cranes, a commercial diver can scrape the guts out of a wreck. The propeller, the rudder, the compass, the portholes and everything else made of lead, copper or brass, are cutout and sold to metal smiths and marine shops. To this breed of diver, a wreck is a piece of precious metal from which he can reap financial gain.

With all these destructive forces combined, very few wrecks survive and hold onto the romantic allure that makes them dreamy. Exceedingly precious is a virgin hull standing upright on a white sand bed with its mast still pointing upwards towards the surface, while fish dance and move fluidly through its interior.

The few wrecks that have remained intact and are not too deep for recreational diving have become famous. And with just a mention in a dive guide, wrecks achieve legendary status. To many islands, a shipwreck can be a wonderful treasure, bearing great potential for additional tourism dollars.

The Windjammer, Bonaire. Opposite page: The Sea Aquarium Tugboats, Curacao

Homage should be paid to Neptune, the god of the sea, for endowing these islands which such marketable commodities.

The Caribbean hold many of these important treasures in their hands. The shipwrecks of the region are precious gems, adding immensely to the pleasure of divers and to the prosperity of dive operators. You can easily see how a wreck like Aruba's Antilla, visited by over five hundred people every day, is of great value. And with more and more divers discovering the beauty of wreck diving, the popularity of these wrecks is steadily increasing.

Unfortunately for these newly initiated wreck divers, there are not many ships sinking these days. With naval wars in decline, sunken military frigates are in dwindling supply. And because freighters use more sophisticated navigational equipment, there are fewer and fewer commercial vessels crashing on the reefs. Dive operators have had to come to terms with the lack of naturally occurring shipwrecks. Most have come to the same solution—buy an old boat and sink it.

In many places in the Caribbean, tourist associations in conjunction with dive operators have taken to creating new shipwrecks. They have sunk military frigates, old freight-ers, planes and even cars. In Grand Cayman they sunk the USS Kittiwake, in Martinique they scuttled the Nahoon and in Curaçao they made a CarPile. All these vessels are sunk near the hotels and not too deep, making them accessible to the dive tourist. In fact now days, a whole commercial industry has been developed around the sinking and creation of shipwrecks.

But these newly sunken ships lack the charm and richness of the old and more genuine wrecks. In fact, new wrecks really don't have much appeal. Time is needed to transform a metallic clipper into a coral colony. Fish need to adopt the ship as their home. Until such time, the wreck looks like a barren and unappealing place.

Like a good cognac, a wreck needs to mature gently in a quiet place before its good taste can be appreciated. And even then, you can never be sure of the outcome. Because of unpredictable factors such as light, plankton growth and current, some wrecks stay desperately void of life. On others, life takes an immediate affinity and the wrecks shortly become fabulous. Take for instance, the LST-467 aka the Wit Shoal in the US Virgin Islands. Sunk in the early 1980s and brushed daily by a good current, the bright orange cup coral that adorns its hulls was prolific from the very start.

Nothing is as wonderful as a good old wreck with a dramatic history that a diver can sense while swimming in the dark hull. The Windjammer in Bonaire captures our imagination and is definitely one of our favorites.

Aboard our sailboat, we sail the Caribbean, looking for dramatic wrecks like the Windjammer. Our particular passion is for historic shipwrecks sitting at depths of between 165 and 300 feet. As wrecks at these depths were until recently inaccessible, there are still plenty of old legendary vessels waiting to be discovered. And vessels at these depths are quite often beautifully virgin—not destroyed by surface waves and current, nor frequently visited by recreational divers. When you land on one such vessel, you really have found a dream wreck.

The evolution of tech diving equipment—mixed gases and re-breathers—has allowed us this pleasure. And as modern diving technology evolves further, the next generation of wreck divers will fuel their quest for discovery with wrecks sitting at even greater depths, going after shipwrecks with even more mysterious allures.

Although some of the spectacular shipwrecks we present in this book have been documented by photographers in the past, even the best wide-angle photography falls short of conveying a complete picture of a vessel. Given the limited visibility underwater, photos can rarely handle the large scale of a wreck. That's why Dominique—after participating for years with l'Equipe Cousteau onboard the Calypso—uses his painterly talents to capture these wrecks in their entire splendor. An original solution, his paintings are a perfect complement to more detail-oriented photo and video images.

In this book we would like to share with you their charm and our passion for these island wrecks. Inside you'll find a real mix of stories, legends, history and just pure visual pleasure. We invite you to experience the pleasure with us.

SS Antilles - Mustique

>> CARIBBEAN SEA
THE VOYAGE

We started our voyage in the south of the Caribbean with the ABC Islands - Aruba, Bonaire and Curacao as well as the atoll of Las Aves in Venezuela. Next we visited the Windward Islands, starting in Grenada and finishing in Martinique. On to the Leeward islands, we slowly made our way from Nevis to the US Virgin Islands. From there we continued our counter clockwise circle, visiting the Bahamas, the Cayman Islands and Honduras.

Though Florida isn't really part of the Caribbean and wasn't part of our journey, we couldn't resist including the wrecks that we visited on a separate journey to West Palm Beach and Boynton Beach during the September mating season of the fantastic creature - the Goliath Grouper.

The shipwrecks we included in this book are those that we found on our journeys. It isn't an exhaustive list of the Dreamwrecks of the Caribbean. This is a work in progress and visits to Barbados, Cuba & Mexico are on our short list of Caribbean hot spots we wish to go to soon!

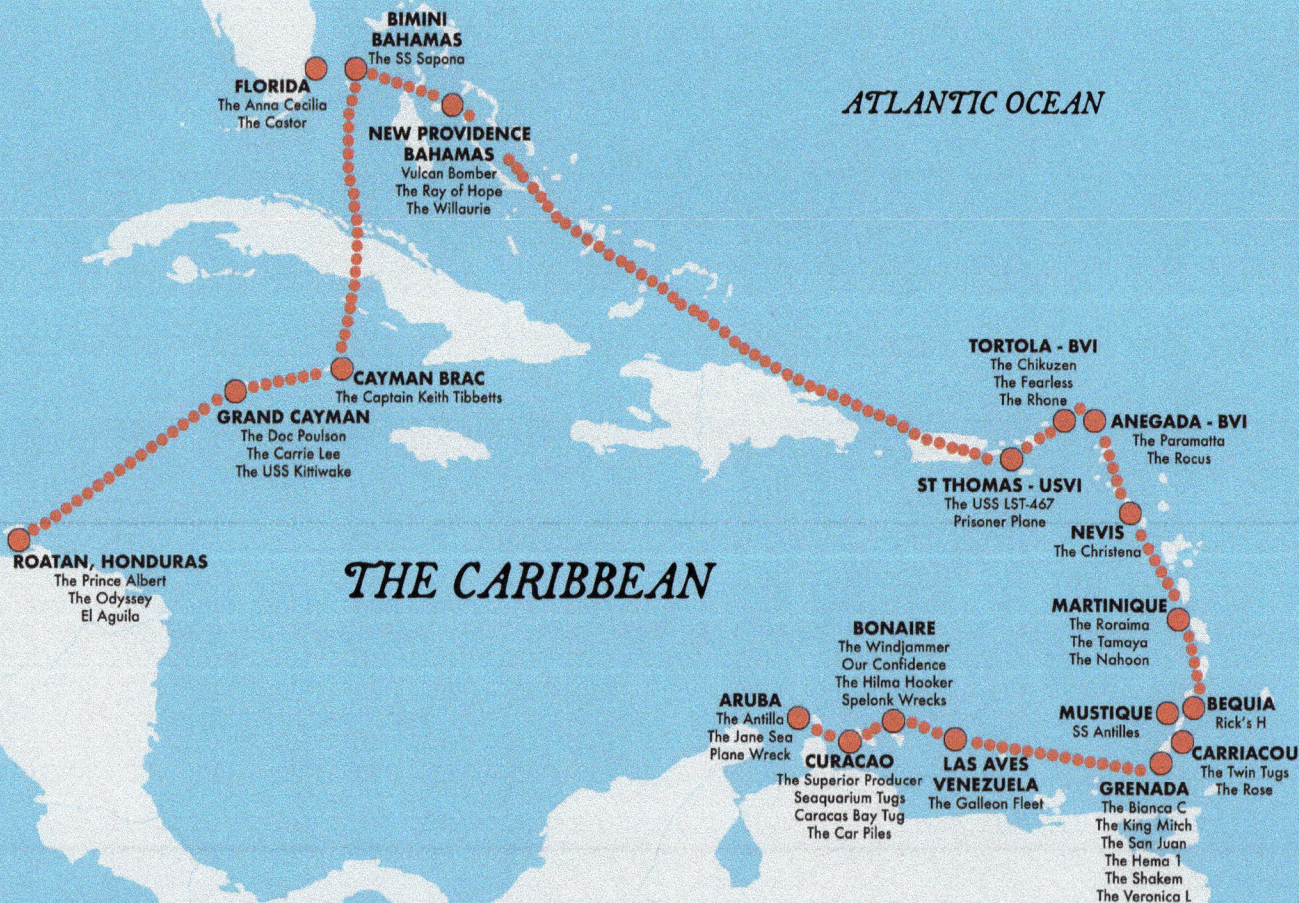

BIMINI
BAHAMAS
The SS Sapona

FLORIDA
The Anna Cecilia
The Castor

ATLANTIC OCEAN

NEW PROVIDENCE
BAHAMAS
Vulcan Bomber
The Ray of Hope
The Willaurie

TORTOLA - BVI
The Chikuzen
The Fearless
The Rhone

ANEGADA - BVI
The Paramatta
The Rocus

CAYMAN BRAC
The Captain Keith Tibbetts

GRAND CAYMAN
The Doc Poulson
The Carrie Lee
The USS Kittiwake

ST THOMAS - USVI
The USS LST-467
Prisoner Plane

NEVIS
The Christena

ROATAN, HONDURAS
The Prince Albert
The Odyssey
El Aguila

THE CARIBBEAN

MARTINIQUE
The Roraima
The Tamaya
The Nahoon

BONAIRE
The Windjammer
Our Confidence
The Hilma Hooker
Spelonk Wrecks

ARUBA
The Antilla
The Jane Sea
Plane Wreck

MUSTIQUE
SS Antilles

BEQUIA
Rick's H

CURACAO
The Superior Producer
Seaquarium Tugs
Caracas Bay Tug
The Car Piles

LAS AVES
VENEZUELA
The Galleon Fleet

CARRIACOU
The Twin Tugs
The Rose

GRENADA
The Bianca C
The King Mitch
The San Juan
The Hema 1
The Shakem
The Veronica L

>> SHIPWRECKS
OF THE CARIBBEAN

1. The Antilla, Aruba 12

2. The Jane Sea, Aruba 16

3. The Plane Wreck, Aruba 18

4. The Superior Producer, Curaçao 19

5. The Caracas Bay Tugboat, Curaçao 23

6. The Sea Aquarium Tugboats, Curaçao 24

7. The Vaersan Bay Tug & Car Piles, Curaçao ... 26

8. The Windjammer, Bonaire, BES Islands 28

9. Our Confidence, Bonaire, BES Islands 36

10. The Hilma Hooker, Bonaire, BES Islands ... 38

11. The Spelonk Wrecks, Bonaire, BES Islands ... 44

12. The Galleon Fleet, Las Aves, Venezuela 46

13. The Bianca C, Grenada 50

14. The King Mitch, Grenada 58

15. The San Juan, Grenada 60

16. The Hema 1, Grenada 62

17. The Shakem, Grenada 64

18. The Veronica L, Grenada 66

19. The Twin Tugs, Carriacou 68

20. The Rose, Carriacou 69

21. The SS Antilles, Mustique, The Grenadines ... 70

22. Rick's H, Bequia, The Grenadines 71

Las Aves Freighter

23. The Tamaya, Martinique 72

24. The Roraima, Martinique 76

25. The Nahoon, Martinique 82

26. The Christena, Nevis 84

27. MS Rocus, Anegada, British Virgin Islands 86

28. Paramatta, Anegada, British Virgin Islands 88

29. RMS Rhone, Tortola, British Virgin Islands 90

30. Chikuzen, Tortola, British Virgin Islands 94

31. The Fearless, Tortola, British Virgin Islands 96

32. USS LST-467, St Thomas, US Virgin Islands 98

33. Prisoner Plane, St Thomas, US Virgin Islands .. 104

34. Ray of Hope, New Providence, Bahamas 105

35. The Willaurie, New Providence, Bahamas 108

36. The SS Sapona, Bimini, Bahamas 110

37. Vulcan Bomber, New Providence, Bahamas ... 112

38. The Captain Keith Tibbetts, Cayman Brac 113

39. The Carrie Lee, Grand Cayman 117

40. The Doc Poulson, Grand Cayman 120

41. The USS Kittiwake, Grand Cayman 122

42. The Prince Albert, Roatan, Honduras 128

43. The Odyssey, Roatan, Honduras 130

44. El Aguila, Roatan, Honduras 132

BONUS WRECKS

45. Anna Cecilia, West Palm Beach, Florida 134

46. The Castor, Boynton Beach, Florida 140

Hema 1 - Grenada

Beneath the surface of the clear Caribbean Sea, close to the spectacular white sand beaches of Aruba, sleep some fabulous historic shipwrecks. The wreck of the Antilla serves as a testimony to the tumultuous past of this beautiful island, dating back to the Second World War.

ARUBA >>THE ANTILLA

Sixty years ago, Aruba wasn't a tourist paradise. There were no hotels or glitzy casinos. No duty-free shops. Instead, Aruba's economy was primarily based around the large oil refinery of San Nicolas at the south end of the island. A short distance from the Venezuelan oil fields of Lake Maracaibo, the Lago and Shell refineries were strategically placed in Aruba.

During the Second World War, Aruba became the fulcrum of oil supply for the Western Hemisphere. From Aruba poured aviation gasoline and motor fuels critical to the Royal Air Force fighters and bombers; for the British Eighth Army guarding the Suez Canal as well as for the growing American military forces. Aruba was charged with keeping American tanks, planes and ships full of fuel and on the move. Producing one out of every sixteen gallons of motor fuel consumed during WWII, Aruba was an important spot on the world map.

Aruba's petroleum complex occupied the attention of the German Third Reich strategists. Even before the first bloodshed in Europe, the secret service of the Aberwher had sent numerous spies to Aruba to plot sabotage missions against the petroleum refineries.

In 1939, the Germans secretly deployed numerous U-boats across the Atlantic to the coast of South America. Five of these submarines were to make the ABC islands their base. Called the Neuland Gruppe, their mission was to attack Aruba and Curaçao's refineries and to torpedo tankers carrying crude oil to the refineries from the Venezuelan oil fields in Lake Maracaibo. Like a pack of gray wolves, the Neuland Gruppe's U-boats crossed the Atlantic. Arriving in the Netherland Antilles, they prowled the waters of Aruba and Curaçao, looking for quiet bays in which to hide and await orders to attack.

Serving as supply boats for these submarines were two big German freighters, circulating in the waters of Aruba. The bigger of the two, the Antilla, was a 400-foot vessel, built in 1938 in Hamburg. Under the guise of a peaceful, commercial freighter working in the neutral waters of the Dutch islands, the Antilla secretly housed all supplies needed for the submarines and their crew, including a deadly arsenal—torpedoes, mines

and other munitions.

In the bars of San Nicolas, the crew of the Antilla spent their evenings fraternizing with Dutch and American soldiers, sailors and petroleum company employees, seeking out delicate details about the oil operations of the island. Charlie's Bar was the hotbed for these spies, where suspicious people traded in false truths while casually sipping their whiskies. But this camaraderie ended the day Adolf Hitler took an aggressive position towards Holland. Without even a declaration of war, Hitler's Wehrmacht attacked Holland, much to the surprise of the Dutch motherland and her colonies.

Suddenly, Germany was officially at war with Holland and the captain of the Antilla feared the repercussions. With the American Navy patrolling the open waters of the Caribbean, the captain hesitated to leave Aruba's coast. Anchored at the northern point of Aruba in a remote inlet called Lighthouse Bay, he felt somewhat sheltered both from the Dutch and from the Americans.

But the Dutch reacted quickly to the German enemy presence. In the middle of the night, rowing silently with their lights dimmed, a team from a small Dutch patrol ship boarded the Antilla. The Dutch demanded the immediate surrender of the ship—leaving the captain

no choice but to comply. In return, the captain asked for VVa few minutes to gather his personal possessions, which the Dutch courteously extended to him.

Taking advantage of this borrowed time, the captain went about sabotaging his ship—overheating the boilers, opening valves, closing drains and, finally, blasting a hole in the side of his freighter. The ship was cut in two and sunk in less than 60 feet of water; the mast and chimney still emerging from the water. Needless to say, the Dutch patrolmen were furious at having being fooled. Having thought they could appropriate the freighter for their own use, they were dumbfounded and pow-

erless as they watched the Antilla sink. The Antilla was unrecoverable.

Meanwhile the war raged on in Europe and thousands of naval soldiers died in the Atlantic and the North Sea. The captain and crew of the Antilla finished the war quietly—imprisoned in a beachfront POW camp in Bonaire that they shared with German civilians, political refugees and Jewish people.

A real paradox, the captain of the Antilla found the Bonairian prison camp so beautiful that after the war he refused to go back to Germany. Instead, he, together with some partners, bought the prison from the Dutch Antilles and built a hotel on the land. Today that hotel is called Divi Flamingo.

To finance the purchase of the land and the construction of the hotel, the captain looked no further than the hull of the Antilla. After the war, the captain went back to his freighter to fetch a very valuable cargo. Still housed in the freighter's infirmary locker were thousands and thousands of vials of morphine, worth a small fortune. This true-life story inspired American author Peter Benchley to write his book The Deep.

The captain of the Antilla gave the dive operators of Aruba a great gift by scuttling his vessel in shallow waters. Lying on a bed of superb white sand, not far away from the coast and protected from the swell, the Antilla is a golden wreck for today's divers, a real war treasure. It is very easy to find, the bow sticking out of the sea. Upon the bow, cormorants, pelicans and sterns regularly perch, looking at the prolific fish population that lurks below, inhabiting the wreck.

Every morning by 10am, an armada of tourist boats comes to the wreck—pirate ships, catamarans, dive boats, glass-bottom boats and even a submarine—bringing hundreds and hundreds of divers and snorkelers daily. The fish of the wreck gather near the surface, waiting to be hand-fed. Yellow-tailed snappers, barracuda, rays and groupers put on quite a show for their supper.

To the blasé, highly experienced wreck diver, the Antilla may appear too easy and commercial. But that's a mistake. Despite all the tourist activity, this wreck has some real choice morsels.

Early in the morning before 10am, between noon and 2pm, or at the end of the day, the wreck is deserted. And it looks grandiose. In the immense hull, the light plays through the portholes. Swarms of silversides fill the cargo hulls, creating elaborate circular forms as they pulsate in unison before your eyes. Between the rigging cables, the shiny silhouettes of barracudas sparkle. It's an absolute pleasure to the eye and to the camera lens.

You can easily be led astray, down the endless corridors of the wreck, where you can still find some locked doors. The spectacular light, deep inside the cargo hulls, evokes great illusions of depth while you are no deeper than 50 feet. You can linger in the labyrinth without worrying about breaking non-decompression tables.

And for treasure seekers, there are still undiscovered artifacts buried in the sand around the wreck, waiting to be exhumed—grenades, munitions, knifes and guns bearing sinister swastikas.

Though a long swim from the shore, the Antilla can be done as a shore dive. Go around noon hour and you can enjoy a quiet moment out at the wreck. But beware of the boat traffic—there is a lot of it. For safety reasons it is a good idea to make yourself visible by carrying a surface marker or other indicator.

The Jane Sea, with it's keel firmly planted on the reef, faces the sometimes strong current. The propeller has been transformed into a bouquet of orange, yellow and red coral polyps.

ARUBA >> THE JANE SEA

The Jane Sea comes alive at night, as our dive lights reveal the colour and beauty of its coral canopy.

Though Aruba's reefs are healthy, with prolific growth of gorgonians and other soft coral, the island lacks the marvellous drop-offs found in both Curaçao and Bonaire. Especially near the hotel zone, where the sand is fine, white and plentiful, there isn't much reef diving to be done. As a result, dive operators in conjunction with the tourist authorities have scuttled many ships. Among the wrecks that have been sunk for the pleasure of divers are the Jane Sea, the Debby II and the Star Gerren. Aruba's reputation for wreck diving is clearly deserved with ships like these making up the diving menu.

The Jane Sea, a 170-foot English freighter, was sunk in 1988 to form an artificial reef. This wreck is an exceptional success—brushed every day by the current, it is covered with gorgonians and orange cup coral. Sitting upright on a sandy bottom near Barcadera Reef, it lies in 100 feet of water. Only accessible by boat, the Jane Sea is well worth a visit and especially for a night dive where the coral on the wreck is all in full blossom.

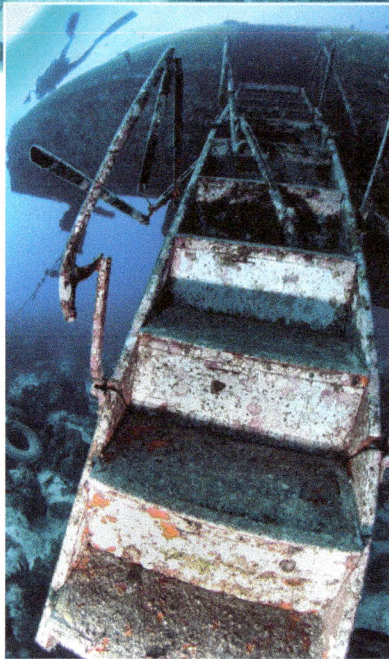

>>ARUBA
THE PLANE WRECK

This airplane wreck is surreal. It rests on its landing gear with its nose pointing in the air, as though it is ready to take off.

Just west of Oranjestad rests a couple of intentionally submerged airplanes.

This NAMC YS-II turboprop passenger airplane belonged to Air Aruba. It was donated to Aruba Water Sports Association and was sunk for divers in 2004. It is completely intact, with its nose resting on the coral reef. The inside is wide open: an invitation to divers with access through the front stairs! This airplane wreck is surreal - it rests on its landing gear and has its nose pointing in the air, as though it is ready to take off for open water from the coral reef.

Close by is the wreck of another plane - a DC-3. This massive plane was destroyed in 1999 by Hurricane Lenny and is now in two pieces. The remains sit on a reef of soft corals and colourful sponges.

>>CURAÇAO
SUPERIOR PRODUCER

The Superior Producer was not a glorious military frigate or a proud sailing vessel. It was a boat with a simple purpose and no real story. Until one Christmas when it sunk.

Some wrecks, even years after their sinking, hold onto the memory of the dramatic events that lead to their demise. Exploded, burned, bombed... you can see how the ship suffered before it sank. That's not the case with the Superior Producer, Curaçao's most famous wreck. It lies on the bottom of the sea, tranquil and intact, like nothing bad ever happened to it—much to the enjoyment of many Curaçao divers. Instead of a horrible tale of woe, the Superior Producer has a funny story. In fact, many people were delighted when this ship sunk.

The little 3000-ton freight-er, flying under a Panama flag, had an easy life. The Superior Producer was not an intrepid military frigate or a glamorous sailing vessel. It traveled from island to island around the Southern Caribbean, picking up and dropping cargo as it went. It was a boat with a simple purpose and not much history.

In September 1977, the Superior Producer arrived in the port of Willemstad to pick up a new cargo. This time, the shipwright was a group of Hindu merchants, looking to make a quick buck. They loaded all they could onto the small freighter—all that they could

sell at a hefty profit for Christmas on the Venezuelan Island of Margarita. They filled the boat with t-shirts, trousers, towels, alcohol and electronic goods. Despite the serious safety warnings of the captain, the merchants stuffed the hulls to the brim, way beyond the capacity of the vessel. With all on board, the Superior Producer left the harbor, entering the Willemstad channel and passing the bridge. With the wind on its side, the ship turned eastward on its bearing towards Margarita.

Back on the Willemstad pier the ship-wrights stared at their ship with great anticipation. Full of hope, they could see a very profitable future within their reach. They blessed the ship with incense.

But suddenly, the little freighter began to roll. From side to side it rocked, taking on water through its portholes. The poorly secured cargo began to move, making the vessel rock more. A passing boat tried to lend a helping hand, towing the Superior Producer back towards the harbor. But the harbormaster, afraid of the half-sunken freighter, ordered a halt to this heroic mission. The ship started to sink.

The crew and the captain jumped into

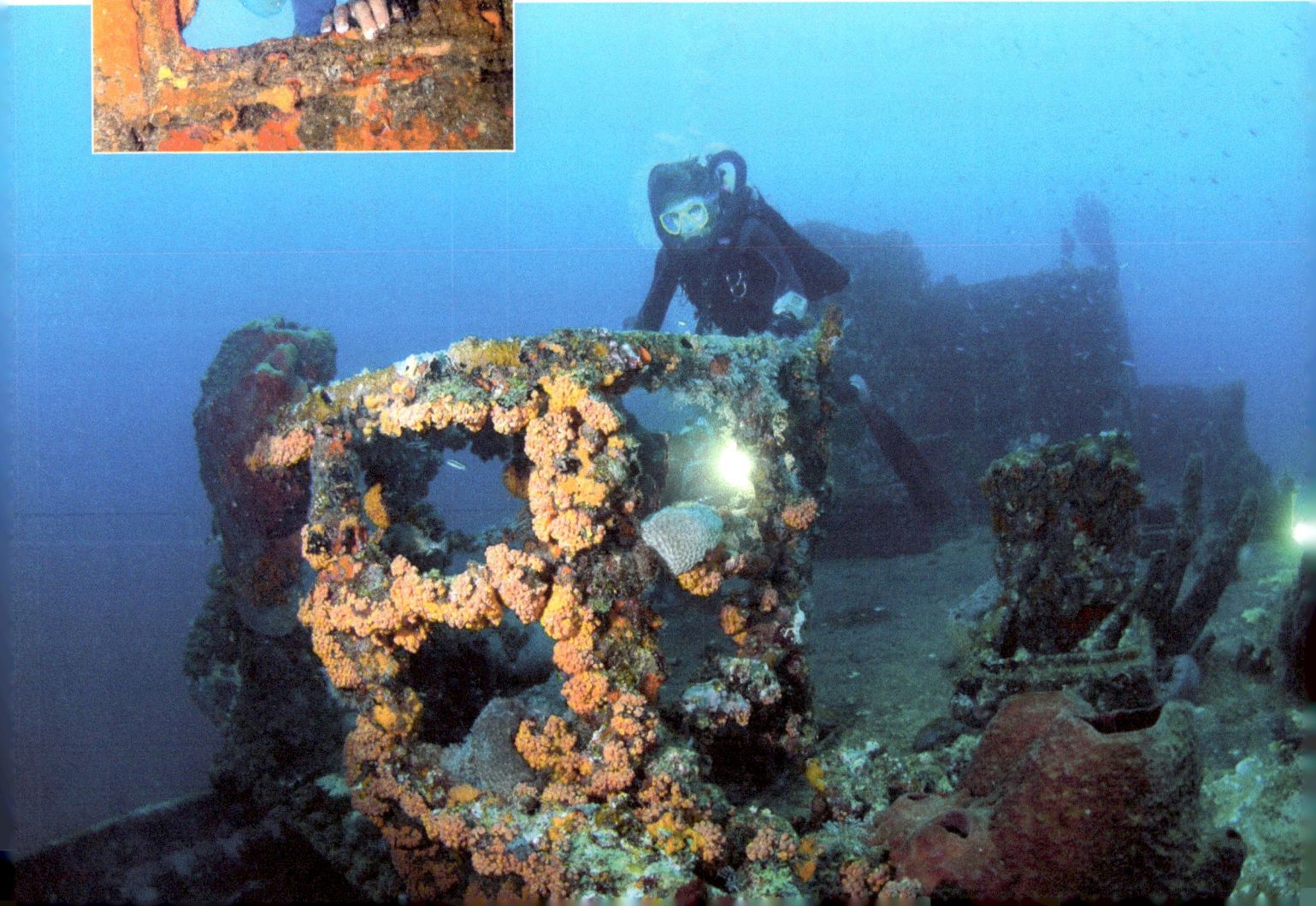

the sea and swam back to the beach, abandoning the sinking vessel. While large eyes looked on from the shore, the Christmas freighter and all the hopes of riches disappeared under the surface of the sea. There was a lot of crying, hollering and lamenting on the pier.

But one person's suffering is quite often another person's joy, and the news of the wreckage echoed through the island of Curaçao. From all parts, people rushed to the scene to help with the "rescue." Not a rescue in the traditional sense, they came to take what they could get. The lucky guys had scuba gear—others just jumped into the water and grabbed anything that they could find floating.

One hundred feet under the surface, divers opened cargo hatches and took out crates of whisky and rum. There was a real craziness in the air, as the rivalry between divers was fierce. For a crate of whisky, masks were flipped off faces and regulators ripped out of mouths. On the beach, there were fights between "rescue" divers and land crew. While divers struggled to get their flippers off, goods were ripped out of their hands. The merchants were more than prepared to fight to get their goods back. The yelling was ear-piercing. Fistfights broke out. All the noise and commotion attracted the police, who confiscated a bottle or two of whisky in passing.

But that wasn't enough to discourage the divers. More and more came—by day and by night. The taste of an easy buck made new divers out of many. Anyone who had a mask and a pair of fins wanted a piece of the action. The dive shops were shopped dry and the few compressors on the island pumped day and night. The only recompression chamber on the island was not enough to care for all the hurried divers.

In just a few days, the wreck was absolutely empty and all the cargo gone, only to reappear some days later on the

market— washed, dried and at a discount price.

Since those crazy days, the wreck has had a peaceful retreat. Placed squarely on its keel, on a sandy coral bottom in 100 feet of water, just 500 feet from the shoreline, the Superior Producer is a pleasure for diver operators and divers alike.

There's nothing more to grab on the wreck—even the portholes have been taken. Over the years, the powerful current has brushed the paint off the hull, and scarlet coral jewels now cover the freighter. The ship has been virtually transformed into a coral garden. Barracudas, jacks and snappers swim quietly in the empty hull where the legendary fights for t-shirts took place. Sometimes, the majestic silhouette of a hammerhead cuts across the mast, sending shivers up your spine. Solidly anchored on the bottom, the Superior Producer has had a happy ending, far away from the lust and greed of humans and the tragedies of the sea.

A new episode to this story potentially threatens the freighter's peaceful rest. In 1999 the Superior Producer's mast— rising to within 15 feet of the surface—was cut off by local harbor authorities who feared that it posed a threat to passing traffic. Then, there was talk about a new pier to be built on the Superior Producer's resting place. Authorities say that the little Curaçao wreck will not be destroyed, but who can say what might happen? Maybe now is the best time to get a good look at this marvelous little wreck.

>>CURAÇAO
CARACAS BAY TUGBOAT

Curaçao is truly the island of tugboat wrecks. This strange little one sunk near the shore in less than 6 meters of water.

A funny little tugboat lies close to the shore of Caracas Bay, in less than 20 feet of water. A small metallic tugboat covered with sponges and coral, it's a perfect wreck for beginners and snorkelers. The fish around the wreck are accustomed to being fed by divers and are very friendly. Sergeant majors, yellow-tailed snappers and bar jacks eagerly await an easy lunch.

On the cliff above sits a big yellow house. Some say it was a haunted house, but it was more likely a quarantine hospital: an isolated place to treat the sick and an easy spot for disposing of dead bodies.

But how did this funny little tugboat sink in such a calm and sheltered spot? A big storm? A fire on board? A torpedo? No. The little tugboat was on the job, docking a big tanker. At the end of the maneuver, the tanker captain dropped the anchor—not in the sea but on the deck of the little tugboat, causing instant rupture and submersion.

On the other side of Caracas Bay, you'll find Curaçao's most spectacular vertical wall. At 130 feet down, look for an interesting ball of cables and chains, home to a very big green moray.

>>CURAÇAO
THE SEA AQUARIUM TUGBOATS

A pair of tugboats with beautiful orange cup coral awaits you at the bottom of the Sea Aquarium wall in Curaçao.

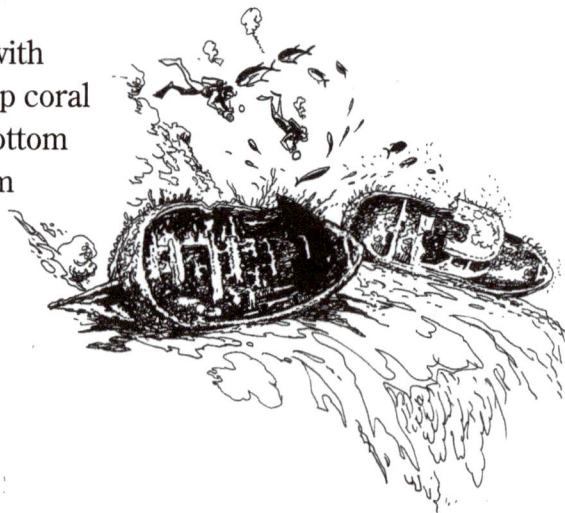

The Seaquarium, built in the early 1990s, is a significant advancement in the underwater landscape of Curaçao. Bring your snorkel gear and jump into the Animal Encounter tank where you'll swim with large groupers, snappers, rainbow parrotfish, cobias and tarpons. Sharks and turtles will brush up against the plexiglass tank to take a good look at you. For anyone wanting to learn about sea life, the Seaquarium is a magical place.

Just outside the walls of the Seaquarium are two tugboats that were sunk to create an artificial reef. However, once sunk, both barges slipped down the drop-off to depths too deep for most recreational divers (165 feet). The Seaquarium plans to lift the two tugboats to shallower depths for the enjoyment of their diving clientele.

The remains of the Oranje Nassau, a large historic steamboat, form part of the Seaquarium's diving attraction.

BEEURK!

NO PARKING

>>CURAÇAO
VAERSEN BAY TUG & CARPILES

If you've ever dreamed of simultaneously diving and driving, this is the place for you.

The strangest wreck in Curaçao has to be the CarPile. If you've ever dreamed of simultaneously diving and driving, this is the place for you. Mountains of cars have been dumped in one spot to make an artificial and very original reef. It's like diving in the middle of a large car crash without any casualties—the fish manage to swim themselves to freedom. If you're a vintage car collector, don't miss this dive. You might find that part you spent years looking for, such as a radiator cap for your old Mercedes. This dive is 65 feet down, right in front of the Princess Beach Hotel.

A second, deeper CarPile exists at Vaersen Bay. Starting at 40 feet and descending down to 165 feet, this second CarPile is more spectacular than the one at Princess Beach. First off, the vintage cars and trucks, which are covered with leaf coral, are more intact. And secondly, on the same dive, you can see the wreck of a 100-foot tugboat. Sitting at 175 feet, this tug is covered with coral and still has a fully intact chimney section. Because it is a bit deep and not many divers visit this wreck, there are plenty of lionfish that have taken up residency on the tugboat.

>>BONAIRE
THE WINDJAMMER

In December 1912, a three-mast clipper named the Mairi Bahn arrived on the island of Bonaire. Little did the captain know that this would be her final port of call.

As told by Dominique Serafini:

In the spring of 1997, I set sail from the Grenadine Islands aboard my catamaran, Blue Manta, in search of spectacular diving and exciting shipwrecks. I sailed westward along the coast of Venezuela, passing the islands of Tortuga, Blanquilla, Margarita and Las Aves. My heading was Bonaire—as I had heard vague references of a magical and virgin wreck sitting just off the island's coast.

Hidden in the back pages of a Skin Diver magazine, I had read an article about a fabulous Bonairian wreck called the Windjammer. And in a lesser-known work by MichaelCrichton—the author of Jurassic Park—there was an entire chapter about Crichton's life-threatening dive experience on the Windjammer. I knew that somewhere off the shores of Bonaire, in about

The Mairi Bhan, Calcutta 1911.

200 feet of water, lay this mysterious clipper, a vessel of magical mystique which has been enticing divers and novelists down to its depths since the late 1960s.

My search for the Windjammer's whereabouts began simply, with inquiries around the island at local dive shops. But my quest turned out to be anything but simple. Much to my surprise, no one seemed to know where I might find this illustrious ship. One elusive answer followed the next. I suspected that I was being kept out of the loop and felt quite estranged, much like a visitor to Transylvania in search of Count Dracula. At the local bookstore, I scanned the pages of several regional dive guides but nowhere was there a reference to the Windjammer. There seemed to be an island-wide blackout on the subject, and

my search for the Windjammer was temporarily dead in its tracks.

Several months later, I would meet a renegade dive operator who was willing to share the whereabouts of the Windjammer and to guide me to that secret spot.

And on a memorable morning, from a secluded part of Bonaire's shoreline, my newfound informant and I made our first dive on the wreck. On the drop-off, at quite a distance from the shore, lay a metallic mast, covered with sponges of many colors. In 30 feet of water, its base pointed towards the deep, indicating the position of the wreck. No doubt, this mast had served as a directional signpost and a seductive force for many divers over the years.

At the base of this mast, we left two extra

tanks, which we had brought for our anticipated decompression stops. Into the deep blue we descended, pulled beyond the reef by a strong current. As we hit 120 feet, from out of nowhere, the ominous silhouette of the large vessel suddenly appeared.

It was breathtaking. Lying on its starboard side in 200 feet of water was the Windjammer. Like the spiny back of a giant reptile, the sharp profile of the keel traced a long line in the white sand. Swimming over the side of the ship, we took a quick glimpse at its impressive hull, waiting for us below. Fifty feet further down on the sand lay the ship's two remaining masts, attached and entangled in their cabling. The bowsprit pointed forward across the sand, with all its rigging intact and hanging. And the rib-like skeleton of the hull, cov-

Left: Maurice Coutts, before his last dive on the Windjammer.
Top Right: Dominique places a memorial plaque on the Windjammer in memory of Maurice.
Middle Right: Cathy and Dominique prepare for one of their many dives on the wreck.

ered with sponges and black coral, was like the door to a haunted house.

I was entranced. Schools of jacks swam the length of the wreck. The beam of my flashlight shined brightly on a big grouper. The sound of our regulators and the allure of our lights had intrigued this peaceful monster, which quickly retreated into the darkness. Two huge barracudas followed closely behind.

But suddenly, the spell was broken—our dive computers, depth gages and chronometers signaled us to our senses. The magical charm of the wreck vanished. It was time to start our ascent to the mast to find our reserve tanks for our lengthy decompression stops.

As I fought against the strong current, pushing me out to sea, I understood the great dangers of this wreck, and why dive operators guarded the whereabouts of the Windjammer with such discretion.

For the untrained diver, the Windjammer is the perfect trap. On some days, with visibility of more than 100 feet, the wreck doesn't seem so deep. And the temptation to go far inside the hull is almost too great to resist. Mix in a little nitrogen narcosis and you don't see the precious time ticking away, nor notice your air being consumed at an unusually high rate. Strong currents pull you away from the coast, far from your decompression tank sitting somewhere back on the reef. This dream wreck could easily become a nightmare.

In my attempts to draw the Windjammer, I have made many dives on this wreck since that first time. Between the short bottom times and the large size of the vessel—239 feet long—it took hundreds of dives to complete my paintings. Most days, I dove the Windjammer alone with a drawing board, sketching the many angles of the ship.

As I penetrated deeper into the hull, I became more and more engrossed in the legends surrounding this mystery ship. Although it had been known for many years as a ghost wreck, I had yet to find the infamous ghost.

Then one day, while inside the hull and completely absorbed in sketching some small detail of the ship, I felt a presence. I heard bubbles that were not mine. Out of the shadow came a white-haired man with cunning blue eyes. A wave of his hand and he was gone into the darkness, leaving nothing behind but a trace of bubbles.

It was an hour later on the shore when I finally met up with this strange visitor. He promptly marched out of the water, sat down next to me, took off his mask and, with a strong Scottish accent, said, "What the hell are you doing on my wreck?"

This is how I met Maurice D. Coutts, a 68-year-old Scotsman from Princeton University in the United States. Maurice, a seasoned diver, had been instrumental in the development of the decompression tables for the British navy. A man of great distinction, he kept company with legendary divers including Jacques Cousteau.

It was in 1968 when Maurice and fellow divers Harry Engelhardt, Percy Sweetnam and Captain Don Stewart first discovered the Windjammer. Each year since, Maurice had made his pilgrimage to Bonaire to spend a month doing nothing else but diving the wreck. Thirty years later when I met Maurice, he knew every square inch of the vessel.

That evening, Maurice asked me if I would accompany him on further dives on the wreck, promising he could show me details of the ship that I had never seen. Naturally, I was elated.

But first, he insisted that I must change my dive equipment to accommodate the additional safety concerns of a 200-foot, 15-minute dive. From that day forward, I dove with two 12-liter tanks on my back and a six-liter tank of oxygen strapped to my bc, which I used to finish up my last decompression stop at 10 feet.

During the first years of our explorations, we could penetrate and swim in the hull which was like a sunken cathedral. One day in 2005, everything changed. The mast that held the hull on its side broke. The metal hull was unstable and tipped over. Luckily, we were not in the wreck when the hull fell. Since that time, the wreck of the Windjammer lies in a new position with the keel raised to the surface. It is now difficult and dangerous to enter the hull. Wrecks age and can suddenly collapse and become a death trap for divers.

He wrote out and handed me the deco stops he had been using for years: 40 feet for 1 minute, 30 feet for 4 minutes, 20 feet for 10 minutes and 10 feet for 23 minutes.

On subsequent dives, he showed me some of the more intimate parts of the Windjammer: the anchor still on the deck, the boiler engines, the last untouched bottle of Italian wine. Typically, we would dive around noon, when the sun's rays penetrated the lattice of the hull, transforming the clipper into an underwater cathedral. The incandescent blue and the shimmering light reminded Maurice of the cathedral in Chartres, France, where he had been as a child.

After the dives, back on the shore, he would crack Scottish jokes and speak of his ancestors fighting at Waterloo against the bloody French. One day, Maurice showed up for our daily dive in a Scottish kilt and cap with a bottle of single-malt in hand. That day we sat on the shore, and he recounted the history of the clipper, which he had pieced together with the help of the insurance records kept by Lloyd's.

For years, Maurice's friend, Captain Don, tried to convince him to stop diving the Windjammer. Don knew that Maurice had suffered a heart attack years back and the risks for the old man were very high. But Don's words fell on deaf ears. Maurice well knew the limits of deep diving, and understood his much-increased health risks. But he chose to continue diving the Windjammer, balancing that risk against his endless passion for the vessel.

On December 2, 1997, after a wonderful dive with Maurice on the wreck, he didn't surface. I finished my 10-foot decompression stop and left the water, waiting for my friend on shore. I eventually found him, one hour later, in 30 feet of water, peacefully lying on a bed of white sand between two coral heads. His mask was on, his eyes open and he had a smile on his face. For a split second, I thought it was another one of his Scottish jokes. But this time it wasn't. The old Scotsman's heart had stopped beating and Maurice lay dead. As there was no sign of panic like a yanked weight belt or a pumped-up bc, I often imagine his death as being quite a peaceful one.

My first impulse was to help Maurice re-

33

turn to his wreck by carrying out and releasing his body into the blue. Though I'm quite sure he would have wanted it that way, I knew it would not be appreciated by his family—or by the police officers who I would later meet on the shore. So I released Maurice's weight belt, inflated his bc, and watched his body float up to the surface. With the help of two fishermen, I brought Maurice's body back to the shore where his dive computer was confiscated and the investigation began. Police officers hoped to unravel the mystery of Maurice's death. Depths and times they discovered but the incalculable passion of an old diver for his wreck, they will never know.

If you ever want to dive the Windjammer, it is up to you to play detective. The surprise is well worth the effort. But be prepared: The depth of the dive combined with frequently strong currents makes it a dive for experienced and well-trained divers. And if you do discover the secluded spot on which the Windjammer lies, don't be alarmed if you meet a ghost. It's just Maurice, making a visit to his Scottish clipper.

>>MORE ABOUT
THE MAIRI BAHN

The Windjammer was one of a series of three-mast iron ships, each designed for speed on the long haul shipping goods between England and India for the MacIntyre Company. Built in Glasgow, Scotland in 1874 by Barclay, Curl and Company, it measured 239 feet long, weighed 378 tons and had a 37-foot beam. Nicknamed the Windjammer, the ship officially sailed under the name the Mairi Bhan, Gaelic for "the Bonnie Mary."

The Windjammer made its maiden voyage from Glasgow to New Zealand in a record seventy-five days. Like the Cutty Sark, the Windjammer was one of the fastest boats ever built. The ship continued its illustrious career, sailing all over the world until 1890.

As the power engine began to revolutionize the shipping industry, many companies such as MacIntyre, vested in sailing ships, had severe financial difficulties. Consequently, the clipper was sold to Bengris & Morzola, an Italian company

CURACAOSCHE COURANT

VRIJDAG den 13n. DECEMBER 1912.

De bemanning van de Italiaansche Brik
Mairi-Bahu is alhier heden ochtend met
den Hollandschen schoener Camia uit
Bonaire aangekomen. Die brik, uit Trinidad met asphaltlading vertrokken, is
ten Westen van de kusten van Bonaire
gezonken. De opvarenden zijn allen gered.

based in Genoa. Without a permanent route to work, the Windjammer moved from port to port, picking up more-or-less legal cargo as it went.

Loaded with olive oil, Italian wines, marble and clothing, the ship set sail on its last trip—from Genoa to Trinidad and then back to Marseilles. While in Trinidad, the ship picked up some unforeseen cargo, namely asphalt, and headed towards the coast of Venezuela.

In December 1905, the ship docked in the port of Kralendijk, Bonaire. The reputation of Captain L. Razeto and his merry band of bandits preceded him and the Bonaire harbormaster ordered the ship out of the harbor.

On December 7, the ship left the port of Kralendijk, hitting the reef at the deserted northern end of the island. How the clipper went aground, no one knows. Was there a fire on board? Severe winds? There are many dramatic versions of the story.

Maurice, who studied the Lloyd's archives, believed the end of the Mairi Bhan to be less dramatic. After forty years of sailing, the clipper was taking on water through the hull rivets. Maurice believed that the weary sea captain chose to run the boat ashore rather than sink at sea. With the Mairi Bhan lodged on the reef, the captain and crew abandoned the ship, carrying all that they could potentially sell.

For Bonairians, the crash of this big clipper was like an early Christmas present. With axes, they salvaged the wood from the bridge, the ropes, the sails, the copper, the nails and the rigging—they skinned the carcass of the old clipper. After several weeks of carnage the main mast fell, killing two people.

Finally in 1912, a hurricane dislodged the Mairi Bhan from the reef and the ship rolled, capsized and sank to the bottom of the sea.

Among fishermen of Rincon, the tale of the Mairi Bhan is still very much alive. Legend says that the ship didn't sink—it simply vanished. One day she will return to the shores of Bonaire, seeking revenge against all those who salvaged parts of her rigging.

Predominantly used as chartered sailing vessels, other clippers of the Windjammer series have sailed the waters of the Caribbean. But in 1999, off the coast of Honduras, the last of the Windjammers mysteriously vanished. Apparently the captain heard of an impending hurricane, leaving his one hundred and fifty passengers at the nearest port to head out to sea with his crew to fight the storm. All that was ever found was a buoy on which the name of the ship—Phantom—was written.

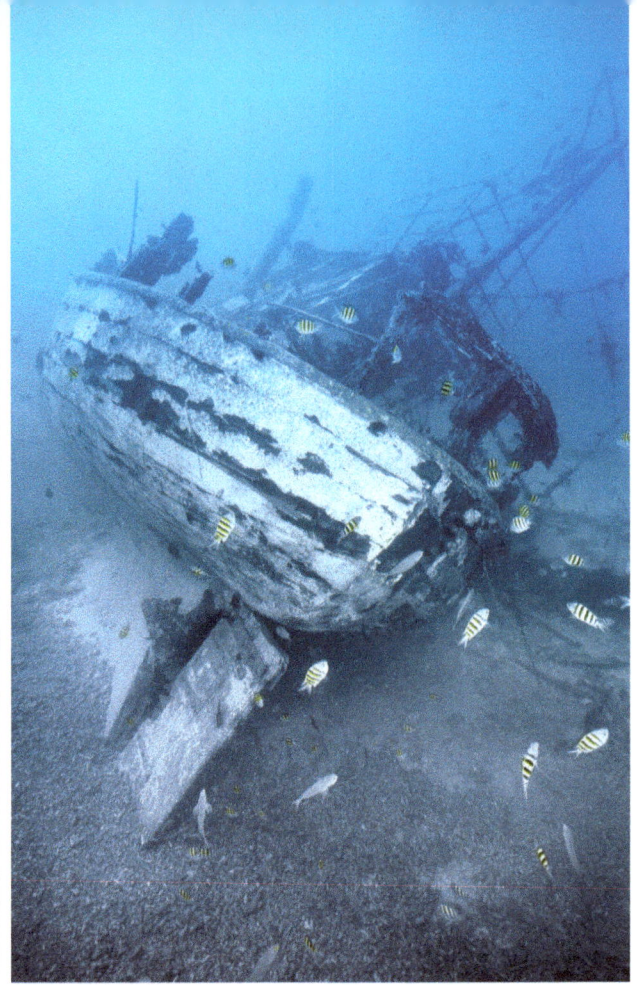

BONAIRE >>OUR CONFIDENCE

Our Confidence, an old Danish wooden boat has ended its life in front of a hotel for the pleasure of divers and fish.

Our Confidence was a 60 foot wooden fishing boat from Denmark. During World War 2, it transported refugees. The ship then moved to the island of Saint Maarten in the Caribbean where it was an inter-island freighter and brought aid to victims of Hurricane Luis in 1995.

In 2003 Our Confidence, unexpectedly sank in front of Harbourvillage Marina in 60 feet of water. The boat began to sink while tied in its slip in the marina. "After trying unsuccessfully to contact authorities, I made the decision to tow the boat out to deeper water," said Harbourvillage Marina Manager Carlos Rodriguez. Our Confidence was towed out of the marina until it began to be weighed down by the water filled hull. The ropes were cut free and the boat descended to its current resting place.

For the first 5 years of its existence, Our Confidence was a spectacular shipwreck. Upright and intact and full of marine life. The wreck was home to goliath groupers, angelfish, moray eels, barracudas and schools of snappers and jacks. We have had much fun free-diving on this wreck, visiting it easily from the boat or shore.

Since that time, the worms have taken their toll and most of the wooden structure is gone.

Cathy takes a last look in the cabin, still intact. Our Confidence crossed the Atlantic, participated in rescue missions and survived a hurricane in Saint Martin. But the wooden hull of this courageous little fishing vessel has not resisted the voracious marine worms.

BONAIRE >>THE HILMA HOOKER

Start with a beautiful Caribbean coral reef. Add some crystal-clear water, a bunch of bandits and a cargo of Colombian contraband. Stir well. The result—an intriguing episode in Bonairian dive history and a wreck called the Hilma Hooker.

One of the major conspirators in this adventure was Captain Don Stewart, an American navigator and scuba diver who sailed into Bonaire in 1961 in search of water and other provisions. Captain Don, a dead-ringer for Errol Flynn, arrived on the Valerie Queen, his two-mast schooner, built in 1912 and sunk in 1963—much to the enjoyment of his Bonairian dive club. For a man of the sea like Captain Don, it would have been unimaginable in 1961 that forty years later, he would still be living in Bonaire.

Back then, Bonaire was a sleepy and forgotten island, with little chance of economic development. Bonaire was the poor sister of the ABC family, and Bonaire natives had little choice but to leave their home in search of employment opportunities. Bonairians were in great demand by the oil refineries of Curaçao and Aruba, as they were well known as good navigators.

Back on the arid island of Bonaire, mostly inhabited by cacti, the rhythm of life was calm and the industrial world, far away. Maybe that's what Captain Don liked so much about it.

Captain Don was quick to identify a fabulous treasure that Bonaire had under its nose. It wasn't gold trinkets or trunks full of jewels and ancient artifacts. It was a living treasure—and hidden but a few feet from the shore. Well-protected on the leeward side of the island in crystal-clear water was a magnificent coral reef.

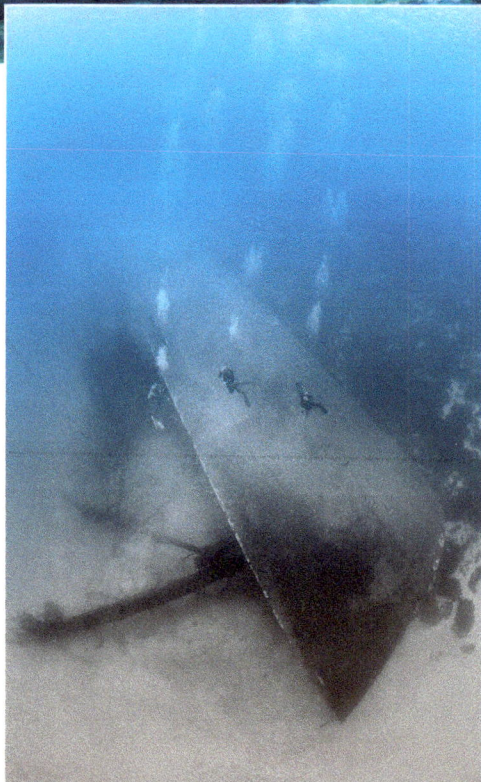

In this hidden corner of the Caribbean, Captain Don set about building bungalows and diving facilities, in hopes of sharing this wonderful treasure with the outside world. He had an original formula: unlimited shore diving, either right in front of the dive center or, thanks to an old truck, at various spots down the coast. Before he knew it, Captain Don had a tourism success story on his hands and dive resorts started popping up all over the island. Dive tourism became a staple of Bonaire's economy.

Bonaire's marvelous reefs were well appreciated by the numerous divers flocking to the island. But there was still one thing missing: a nice wreck, not too far away from the shore and not too deep.

There were already plenty of shipwrecks along the coastline of Bonaire. The Valerie Queen, Captain Don's sailboat, lay on the reef in front of his hotel, but the wooden structure had not withstood the voracious worms that ate away at the hull.

There was also the Windjammer, the superb three-mast clipper—however it was sunk in water far too deep for most recreational divers. Thus begins the story of the Hilma Hooker.

In April 1984, suffering from mechanical problems and enroute for some unknown destination, a Colombian cargo ship by the name of the Hilma Hooker sought refuge on the island of Bonaire. The vessel threw its anchor at a distance from the shore, close to Klein Bonaire—the little islet on the leeward side of Bonaire.

Customs officials watched the freighter from the shoreline of Bonaire. Why was the Hilma Hooker hiding behind Klein Bonaire, avoiding docking in the Kralendijk harbor? What was the reason for such irregular and suspicious behavior? So out to Klein Bonaire the officers went, demanding permission to board the vessel and inspect its cargo.

Without any real option, the captain reluctantly let the authorities aboard. But

no sooner had the officers planted their feet on the deck, than the captain pulled up his anchor, letting the ship drift out towards international waters. The customs officials retaliated by towing the Hilma Hooker into the port of Kralendijk, stopping the freighter from making its grand escape. The captain protested furiously, but his complaints fell on deaf ears.

Once docked in the port, customs officials started their rigorous inspection of the ship. In fact, they shipped a team of investigative specialists in from Miami for the purpose. But despite all the expert advice, the officials finished their search humiliated and empty-handed. Convinced that something was wrong, they asked Captain Don for his help. Using scuba gear, Don and his friend Janet scoured the bottom of the bottom of the ship and quickly found a suspicious metal plate welded to the hull. The captain had no doubt made a sort of secret compartment, perhaps to

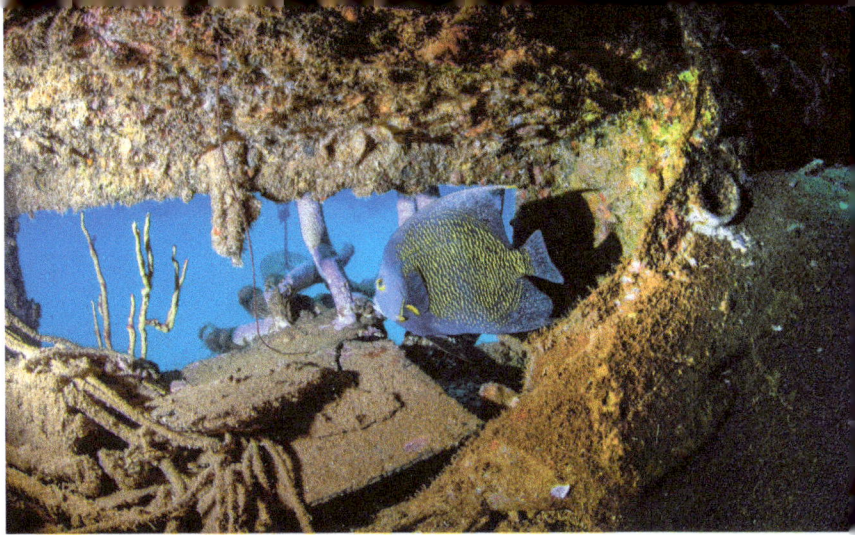

hide some mystery stash.

As the search narrowed, the captain tried one last maneuver to sabotage the investigation. Discretely, he opened the Hooker's floodgates so as to scuttle the ship, but unfortunately a bit too late. Behind the hidden bulkhead, the inspectors found the pot of gold—a nice package of marijuana and cocaine. Twelve tons to be exact.

With the captain in jail and the ship seized, officers tried to find the boat's owner, but to no avail—the Hooker was left unclaimed, abandoned in the port. The ship posed a great problem to the port authorities. What were they to do with this old freighter taking on water and needing to be pumped continuously?

The Hooker was a ship that clearly risked sinking and could potentially block other commercial vessels from docking at the port. The weeks passed. Not knowing what to do with this rusty old vessel, the file passed from one administrator's desk to another.

But the diving establishment of Bonaire had a very clear idea of what to do with the Hilma Hooker—and hatched a scheme to get their way. As a service to the port authorities, members of the dive community proposed to tow the Hilma Hooker out of the Kralendijk harbor and out of the hair of the port authorities. They suggested towing the vessel to the south end of the island, where it would be of less risk if it happened to sink.

After much debate, the port authorities accepted the proposal and the old tired freighter was towed out to what would be its final resting-place.

Anchored in the fine white sand near Pink Beach, the Hilma Hooker stoically awaited her destiny.

On September 12, 1984, with the help by a few finned conspirators, the cargo ship mysteriously sunk. Anchors attached, the hull sits at 100 feet on a bed of sand between two coral reefs. Who could dream of a better spot for a superb underwater attraction?

It's pointless to dive the Hilma Hooker from a boat. As the wreck is easily accessible from the shore, just rent a pick-up and head down the coast. Look for a yellow rock on the shore with "Hilma Hooker" written on it and park. Fins in hand and a tank on your back, you can easily walk right into the water.

The Hilma Hooker is by far the most popular dive site in Bonaire and thousands come every year to dive it. By 10am, the action begins. The shoreline late in the morning looks more like a parking lot than a secluded island paradise. Underwater, the hull of the ship bubbles and dozens of silvery garlands of air stream up to the surface. Small groups of divers cross every which way in the slipway.

Show up early in the morning, before the crowds arrive, and you can peacefully enjoy the splendor of the fish that inhabit this underwater condominium. You'll see parrotfish, groupers, snappers and wrasses. But most exceptionally, you'll see the glittery tarpons that patrol the sides of the freighter and then disappear into the shadows.

43

BONAIRE >>THE SPELUNK WRECKS

If you're not afraid of the wind and current, try your luck on the windward side for some of the lesser-known shipwrecks and other surprises.

If you are in Bonaire during the months of September, October or November, take advantage of the seasonal lull in the wind to dive the windward side of the islands. This is the only time of the year when windward-side diving is a real possibility. But be prepared because even during these fall months, the current remains very strong and access to the various dive sites by the shore is quite dangerous. In short, diving the windward side is a real expedition.

So why bother? For the adventurous div-er, the wild side of the ABC islands has much to offer. Groupers, snappers, turtles, spotted eagle rays, manta rays, sharks and lobsters are much more plentiful and larger in size than those you find on the leeward side. On the windward side, the ocean's forces have done a marvelous job of protecting marine species from human intervention—at least as good as any marine park does.

Having a manta ray swim up while you're snorkeling on the surface, finding a school of two hundred tarpons, swimming with nurse sharks, or watching a school of Atlantic spade-fish—these are the type of fantastic experi-ence that the windward coast has to offer.

The windward side of Bonaire also has plenty of undiscovered wrecks. Often, ships suffering from motor or navigational problems are carried by the waves towards the shoreline and crash on the coast. And as the windward side is pretty much uninhabited, a ship can easily sink with no one the wiser.

These wrecks are nothing like leeward-side wrecks. Lacking the protection from the waves and the swell that the leeward side provides, their remains rapidly become scattered along the rocky bottom and disappear. Today's shipwreck can be gone tomorrow. And tomorrow a new shipwreck can magically appear.

There are a few places where the coastline permits shore diving, but most often, a shore dive on the windward side implies jumping off the cliff, like some local fishermen do. This style of stunt diving can be quite dangerous, especially when it comes to getting back out of the water, with the waves crashing down on the rocky shoreline. Despite all these inconveniences, wild side diving is an exhilarating experience that any courageous, adventure-seeking person can't miss.

Just off the coast of Sorobon, out past the windsurfers and before the drop-off, is a 30-foot aquarium-like enclave, called Blue Hole. With a sand base and light turquoise water, Blue Hole is a beautiful oasis. Perhaps Bonaire's best-known windward site, this is a place where tarpons, turtles, nurse sharks and rays hide out and where fish are incredibly plentiful. As Blue Hole is very shallow, it's an excellent free-diving site. With just a mask, snorkel and fins you can have a wonderful encounter with marine life—much more intimate than with noisy scuba equipment. Blue Hole can be done as a shore dive by swimming out from the old shrimp factory or by boat.

On the other side of Lac Bay is the Cai boat channel. There lives an enormous group of tarpons. If you find yourself alone, at a depth of about 40 feet, as many as two hundred tarpons will make circles around you. Out on the reef are turtles and, depending on the time of the year, a school of eagle ray. After the reef bottoms out, down on the sand at 230 feet you will find the wreck of a fishing vessel called Zen.

Further to the north, at the base of the old Spelonk lighthouse, is a veritable graveyard of shipwrecks. There lie the remains of four boats—a wooden sailboat, a fiberglass sailboat, a metal-hulled freighter and a fishing boat.

Most picturesque is the fishing boat, whose interior is covered by beautiful red gor-

gonians. Still very much intact, this fishing vessel sunk within meters of a 200-foot freighter that had sunk on the spot many decades before. The large freighter was more than likely a late-nineteenth-century fishing vessel, given the small-sized openings of the cargo hulls. Found near this wreck, lying on the sand, was a bunch of clear glass tubes—perhaps a clue to the mystery of this vessel. The atmosphere surrounding these wrecks is very dramatic, with immense boulders on a bed of sand as well as tunnels and caves burrowed into the side of the cliff.

Diving Spelonk can be done from the shore—the entry and especially the exit are quite treacherous, but you can get in the water at Boca Spelonk. However, if you want to see the Spelonk wrecks, which are around the corner from Boca Spelonk, you must do it from a boat.

South of Lac Bay, you'll find some easier shore dives. Though the reef isn't too dramatic, Baby Beach and the reef in front of the old shrimp factory provide great chances for spotting nurse sharks and rays. And the soft coral formations in front of Willemstoren lighthouse are spectacular.

LAS AVES
SOTAVENTO

Lighthouse Island

Long Island

TANKER

Round Island

FREIGHTER

Mangrove Island

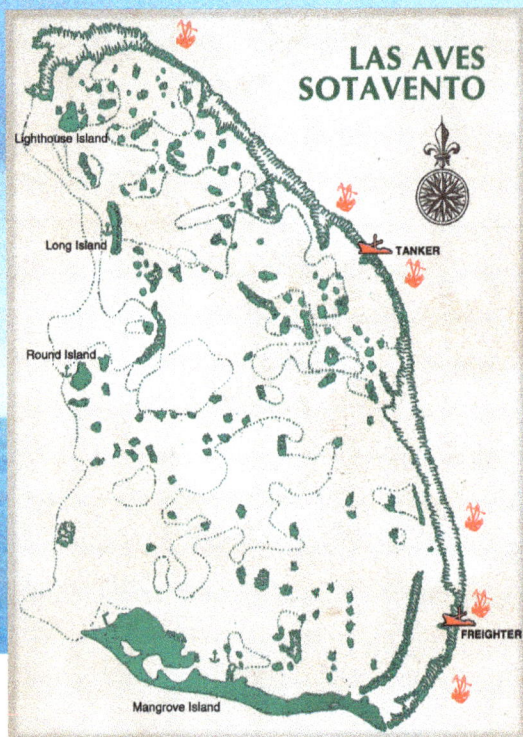

LAS AVES >>THE GALLEON FLEET

Forty miles east of Bonaire, a large semi-submerged coral reef faintly peeps above the surface of the sea. This very dangerous and practically invisible reef has been known for centuries as a navigational trap. In its coral clutches lie the remains of an expedition by the French that could have changed the destiny of the southern Caribbean.

Though officially not part of the ABC islands, any book about the history of the ABCs wouldn't be complete without a few words about the Archipelago of Las Aves. This spectacular Venezuelan coral atoll is a real hot spot for shipwrecks and a major component in the history of Aruba, Bonaire and Curaçao.

To get to Las Aves you'll need a handful of courage and a bowl of very thick porridge in your gut. Only accessible by boat, Las Aves

is a twenty-hour sail from the southern tip of Bonaire. Once past the island of Bonaire, it's high, wide-open sea all the way—and worse, it's sailing completely against the waves. The southwesterly wind of Alezes blows directly opposite your course, forcing you to tack as many as twenty times during the trip.

On the horizon, Las Aves is almost invisible. In the south, you can vaguely make out an island, which closes Las Aves' hidden cres-

cent-shaped reef at its southernmost tip. As you get a bit closer, several other islands come into view. On the western side, Las Aves' few barren sandbar islands provide shelter from the wind and waves—and a comfortable place to anchor a boat.

But shipwreck hunters don't stop there. In search of sunken vessels, you need to cross Las Aves' lagoon, avoiding large coral patches the length of the trip. Colors change from

turquoise to green-blue to deep-blue as you work your way through this liquid maze. Clear on the other side of the lagoon is a true barrier reef, with a solid line of white waves crashing down on the coral, which peeps just above the surface. On the breakpoint are the silhouettes of two ships: Like sentinels, a wrecked tanker to the north and a sunken freighter to the south stand above the waterline on the barrier reef. They are clear reminders of the potential dangers this hidden reef poses to ships arriving from the east.

On this reef, encrusted in coral, lie dozens of cannons, anchors, chains and metal pieces from seventeenth-century vessels. These are the remaining vestiges of twelve French galleons that sunk in Las Aves in 1678.

In the late 1600s a campaign of battles was fought throughout the Caribbean for the colonial occupation of the islands. The French won many victories against the English. Under the direction of Admiral d'Estrées, the French easily captured the colonies of St Lucia, St Vincent, Grenada and Trinidad. In 1678, by order of the King of France, d'Estrées was sent on a mission to conquer the Dutch-occupied islands of Bonaire and Curaçao.

To the French, the expedition seemed a simple one. D'Estrées, intoxicated by his prior victories in the north, was sure the Dutch would crumble with just a few cannon shots. With a well-planned attack and a fleet of eighteen vessels and thousands of men, the odds would be in his favor. For added firepower, he invited pirate and mercenary ships to join the expedition, promising them part of the loot. Looking for a conclusive victory, d'Estrées didn't realize that in amongst the mercenaries were a few Dutch spies.

And so, with his elaborate plan, d'Estrées' fleet set sail from Trinidad. The wind pushed the armada along the coast of Venezuela and past the Archipelago of Los Roques towards Bonaire.

Informed of the oncoming danger, Dutch officials knew they were facing a potential disaster, as their army in Curaçao was too weak to resist such a large attack by the French. But Holland was definitely not prepared to surrender these prize islands, which furnished salt to the fisheries.

Confident in their superior knowledge of the southern Caribbean as well as their excellent seamanship, the Dutch laid their trap. D'Estrées, lacking in sailing experience and far too confident, was to be an easy mark.

A small fleet of Dutch boats set sail from Curaçao destined for Las Aves. Once assembled on the Venezuelan archipelago, the Dutch maneuvered their ships into the heart of Las Aves' lagoon and waited for the arrival of the French, en route to Bonaire. As night fell, lanterns were lit. Simulating the lights of a town, the Dutch sailors hoped to convince the French that they had reached Bonaire. In so doing, they could attract the French galleons onto the reef.

As the French fleet approached Las Aves, d'Estrées' vigil spotted the lights. Against the advice of his captains and navigators, the Admiral headed his ship—le Terrible—straight for the trap and directly towards the coral reef. By the time the breakers were spotted, it was too late. Le Terrible, too heavy to veer into the wind, couldn't avoid the reef.

To warn the rest of the armada, le Terrible fired its cannon. But the signal was misinterpreted as a call for help, and one by one, the rest of the boats in the fleet headed towards the reef. Pushed forward by the waves, the vessels touched bottom and implanted themselves in the reef, without a chance of breaking free.

A few vessels had time to veer away. One ship was able to rescue d'Estrées and many of his senior officers, avoiding their capture by the Dutch. The vessel beat a hasty retreat from Las Aves, abandoning a thousand or more soldiers, condemning them to a slow death on the reef or capture by the Dutch.

Back in France, accused of abandoning his men, d'Estrées was court-martialed. But given his tight relations with the French nobility, he wasn't condemned. Soon after, a peace treaty was signed between the Dutch, French, English and Spanish regarding the islands of the Caribbean. And the Dutch kept their colonies of Aruba, Bonaire and Curaçao.

Perhaps, if the Admiral had been more cunning, we all might have ended up in Bonaire under the French flag, eating steak-frit while drinking red wine and playing the accordion.

This page in the history of the French navy is not a glorious one and has all but been forgotten. Very little documentation of the expedition still exists. The extracts of the court case were preserved and are at the Musée de la Marine in Paris. That's where we found an officer's testimony together with an extremely precise map of where the twelve vessels sunk on the reef.

Over the years, there have been many wreck-hunting expeditions to Las Aves. Explorers have come and gone in vain, searching for galleon treasures. It isn't the extreme underwater depths that posses the difficulties. On the contrary, it is the fact that there is hardly any water. The relics are close to the surface where the coral grows most prolifically and where the waves break hard, making underwater exploration and recovery very difficult. In fact many expeditions have ended with broken teeth.

Nowhere else in the Caribbean can you find so many seventeenth-century galleon relics. On

most other islands, wreck hunters have tampered with or removed these rare gems.

In Las Aves, anchors, cannons and other boat parts are spread out over an immense surface area of about seven miles. Imagine how many relics exist, given that on le Terrible alone there were seventy cannons of differing size. In a forest of staghorn coral and covered by fire coral, it really takes a well-tuned eye to be able to distinguish the artifacts from dead pieces of coral.

The largest cannon that we found was completely by fluke—when Dominique stood up on the rubble bed below. While staring down at his fins, Catherine's eyes were drawn to the nine-foot cannon that he was standing on.

In the course of our search, we found many cannons but all of them iron. The large bronze cannons, which were on board the French fleet, were more than likely removed by the Dutch after the ambush—with the "help" of the captured French soldiers.

Of the thirteen vessels that hit the reef, one managed to disengage. But while trying to make an evasive turn around the reef, it sank in deeper water. To reach this wreck you must cross to the outside of the reef, passing a labyrinth of coral while fighting the breakers. This isn't a small adventure and can often be acrobatic.

Your other choice is to wait until the wind dies down and then leisurely swim across the reef. That's our preferred method. With our cat-

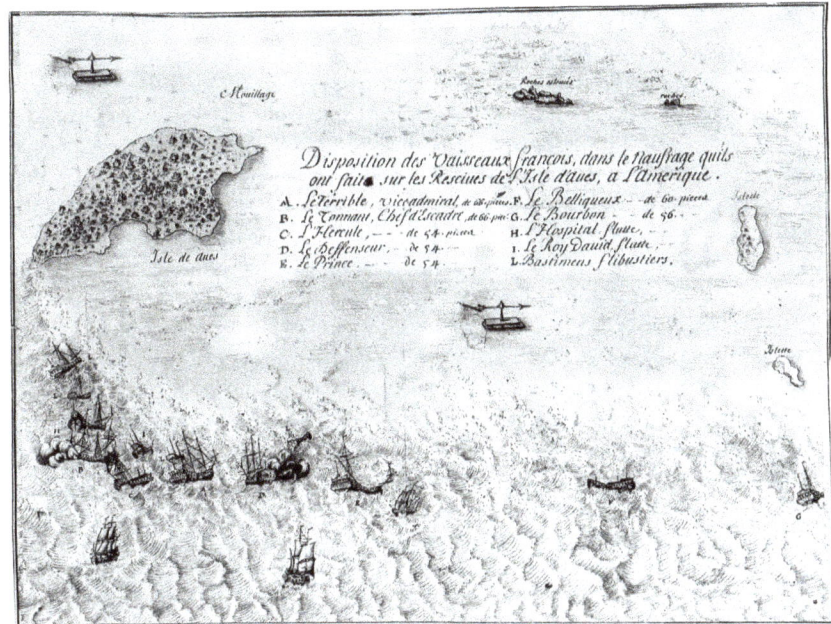

Map of the wrecks from an officer's testimony. Archives of Musée de la Marine in Paris.

amaran anchored in the lagoon, we wait, completely losing track of time.

For us, like the Admiral, Las Aves is a trap. We are trapped by the marvels of the place and return often. Las Aves has purity, tranquility and beauty, not to mention the bands of large fish and the gorgeous coral formations. It's a real treasure that has no price. During one of our visits, a curious seven-foot barracu-

da started living under the catamaran, waiting for the scraps off our plates. "Monsieur Jules" quickly becomes a part of daily life every time we return.

You see, Las Aves is one of the last remaining virgin sanctuaries in the Caribbean, not touched by tourism. Searching for anchors and cannons becomes just a pretense for being there.

GRENADA >>THE BIANCA C

In October 1961, 362 cruise ship passengers found themselves on the docks of St George, Grenada, in their pyjamas, wondering what had happened to their Caribbean cruise.

For the cruise ship passengers of the Bianca C, their port call in Grenada was going to be an experience they would never forget.

The morning of Octobers 22, 1961, Bianca C, a Costa Line cruise ship, was about to anchor near the town of Saint George in Grenada when there were a series of explosions onboard. The captain quickly disembarked the passengers with the help of local rescue and fishing boats. Thanks to the speed of the maneuver, there were no casualties. The 362 passengers, not really knowing what was going on, found themselves in their pyjamas on the quays of St. George!

The Costa Line's steamer was smouldering and smoking. For fear that the vessel might sink in the harbour, the burning vessel was towed by an English frigate toward the Pointe de Saline. But the wind disrupted

the rescuers' program. As the vessel left the harbour, gusts of wind shifted everything. The tow line broke and the giant cruise drifted off. The Bianca C cracked in two and began to sink. In a whirlwind of flames and smoke, the carcass disappeared beneath the surface a few miles off the Pointe des Salines.

The story of the sinking of the Bianca C is very much part of local folklore. Ask anyone on the island. Everyone in Grenada knows someone who helped with the rescue of the passengers. The owner of the Bianca C wanted to than the inhabitants of Grenada and gave the island a monument to commemorate the event. Standing at the harbour is the statue of a Christ.

Years passed, and time forgot the Bianca C until the day local divers rediscovered the wreck, laying on a sandy bottom at 200 feet. Initially it was the salvage-driven divers that were interested in the vessel. The first visitors went in search of dinner plates, silver cutlery and bronze ornaments. They also went in search of the wine cellar where there was champagne, wine, cognac and whiskey. Hundreds of bottles of whisky were still stocked inside. Several divers disappeared in the dark holds in search of the treasures on board and the cellar with spirits. Some did not return.

A visit of the wreck does not, at first, appear difficult because the bridge of Bianca C is barely at 110 feet. But the current is quite often strong on the wreck and that complicates things. The dives are generally drift dives with a surface buoy. And to cover the full 536 feet of the deck, you have to be very good on air. In fact, several sequential dives (with long surface intervals) are necessary to discover this immense wreck. The rear of the ship, where the explosion took place is turned to port. The swimming pool is still full, but now have fish swimming in it. The corridors of the ship make for mysterious dark labyrinths.

Shelter inside the twisted metal bow you can escape the current, From the ship's bridge, you can gaze out in the blue at eagle rays and schools of barracudas swimming the length of the wreck . On the sand, at 200 feet in front of the ship lies the anchors. If you turn and face the bow, it is quite an incredible site - the impressive gigantic dark bow of the ship, covered with

large purple gorgonians and coral whips against the sunny surface light.

It has been in the company of Peter and Gerlinda Seupel of Aquanauts Grenada that we have been able to do multiple dives on this wreck to do photography and painting. You can never grow tired of the Bianca C, as there is always something new to see on the wreck, a new corner to explore.

Diving on the Bianca C is not a year-round activity. When the current draws the waters of the Orinoco to Grenada, the wreck disappears in a greenish mist. It's time to put away your fins and go to the library to study the mysterious and tumultuous history of the Bianca C. Because the Bianca C, sailing under the Italian flag, was once a French vessel!

The construction of the large cruise ship, a Messageries Martimes project, begun in December 1938, with plans for a quick turnaround. Alas, history didn't follow the established plan. The works begun at La Ciotat but was interrupted by the declaratory war of 1939, by the fall of the government and the occupation of France by the Nazis. The construction was supervised of the German officers of the Kriegsmarine.

The french workers sabotaged and blocked the construction of the ship. The exasperated German officers took hostages to put an end to the strikes until such a time that the hull was finished.

During the collaborative period, the Vichy government and the German authorities named the liner Marechal Pétain. Marechal, here we are! You, the savior of France! Pom ... popom! And it was with these pompous and nauseating innuendos that on June 10, 1944, this great modern liner was launched... two days after the landing of Normandy!

Towed from La Ciotat to the Etang de Berre, Mare-

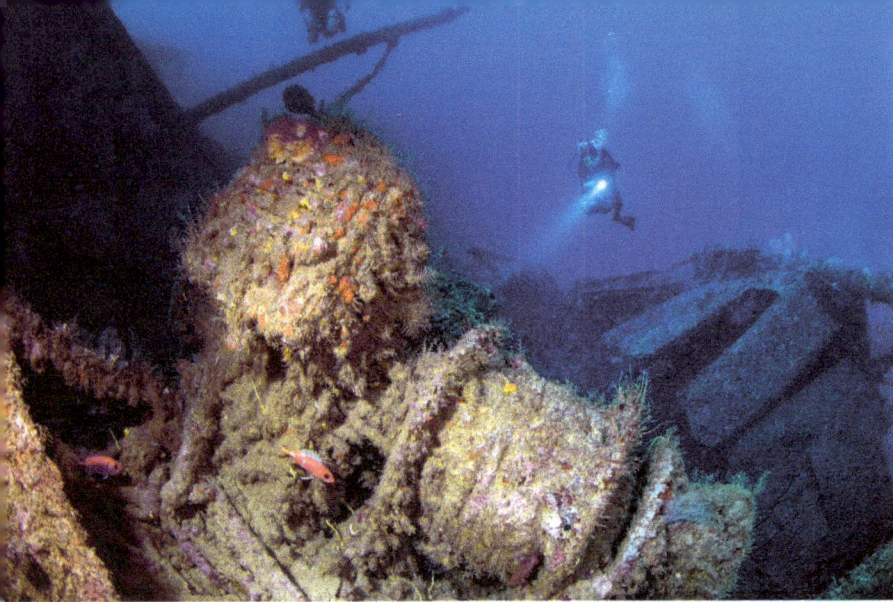

sea-worthy.

Ten years after signing the original construction order, the Compagnie des Messageries Maritime finally got its beautiful steamer, renamed La Marseillaise.

On April 18, 1949, La Marseillaise made its first cruise, heading towards Indochina. On September 5th, the ship reached Saigon. Luxuriously designed and equipped with powerful 31,000 hp engines, "La Marseillais" could reach 20 knots. She became the flagship of the company. 536 feet long, 75 feet wide, it could hold 341 passengers in first class and 302 passengers in economy.

In 1954, Indochina gained independence and La Marseillaise needed to change its route once again, resuming service to the Mediterranean. The ship brought passengers to Alexandria until September 1956 when the Suez Canal crisis broke out. The liner was requisitioned to serve as a hospital ship, transporting troops to Limassol and Bizerte, until its return to Marseilles in February 1957.

La Marseillaise was put up for sale. Purchased by an Italian, the boat's names was changed to Arosa Sky. Reshaped, it returned to service, this time with an Atlantic route. In June 1958, the Arosa Sky headed to New York but a fire broke out on board. The ship started to appear cursed and the Italian owner decided it best to break free and auction off the ship.

The Costa Line bought the boat and the boat went back again to the shipyard, this time to change its silhouette and repainted the hull white. On 2 March 1959, the

chal Pétain could not take the sea and remained at the wharf until the end of the war. As the European fortress cracked under the battering by the allies, the glorious Marechal sought exile with his clique of frightening Germany collaborators, before being subjected to the judgment of history and imprisoned until the end of his life at the island of Yeu.

Still in La Ciotat, on August 21, 1944, the ship's mooring lines broke and it started drifting, crashing into a railway bridge. Badly damaged, it went back to the dry dock in La Ciotat and it was not until 1949 that the ship was

THE BIANCA C

The Corridor

The Chimney

The Bridge

The Stern Winch

The Forecastle

The Pool

The Gangway

The Bow

The Anchor

cruiseship began its new career with a new name - the Bianca C. It sailed from Genoa to the Caribbean and onto New York. The Bianca C arrived in New York on Dec 22, 1959. After a year or so, cruises in the Caribbean really started to become successful. It seemed that the Bianca C had finally hit its stride... until that morning in October 1961, when it sank in Grenada in a ball of flames.

Since that time, the former Maréchal Pétain, La Marseillaise, Arosa Sky, and Bianca C has had its last name change. This time it is the divers who continue to visit the wreck who have baptized the ship - The Titanic of the Caribbean - a name that will always have and that suits it well.

GRENADA >>THE KING MITCH

The Atlantic side of Grenada is home to several world-class shipwrecks and one of the best is the King Mitch.

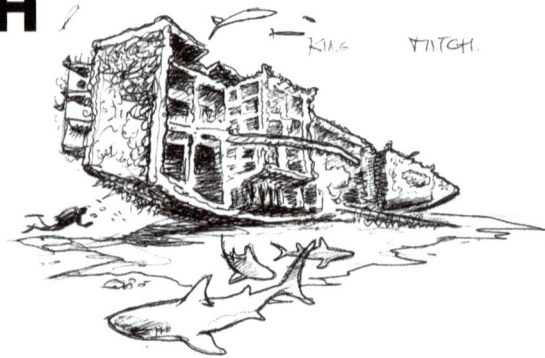

The Atlantic nautical crossing between Grenada and Trinidad in principle seems easy. It's a short trip - only 100 miles. But in the channel between the islands, the currents and the wind can make the conditions difficult. It's a region that can have rough seas, big swells and nasty short waves that smash against the hulls of ships making the passage. There are quite a few shipwrecks, not far from Grenada, that have become dramatic habitats for marine life. Though many have still not been discovered, there is one 4 miles offshore we know of - a notorious one called the King Mitch.

This is a big wreck - 240 feet from bow to stern. Originally the King Mitch was a US

Navy minesweeper that served in WWII. Once it was decommissioned, the ship was converted into a freighter with two cargo holds and a crane attached to the deck in its midsection. The ship finished its life hauling cement between Grenada and Trinidad. With a boxy stern and a pointy bow, it is definitely an unusual ship and looks nothing like a minesweeper and only marginally like a cargo vessel.

King Mitch lies on its port side in 110 feet of water. It sank in 1981 when the bilge pump failed. Luckily all the crew survived. There is some coral growth and gorgonians on the hull, but the growth is nowhere near as prolific as wrecks on the Caribbean side. What the King Mitch does have is lots of is nurse sharks. In the holds, sleeping sharks rest and lobsters hide amongst the cement that sank along with the ship. With a very slow approach, one can spend some quality time watching the nurse sharks.

Atlantic-side shipwrecks can only be visited in ideal conditions. The wrecks in general are in exposed locations and between the really strong currents underwater and the surface swells, the dive can be very technical. You need a good dive shop and Aquanauts Grenada, run by Peter Seupel, is one of the best

in the Caribbean. Their boat is great and they have an experienced and well-trained team.

Following a GPS coordinate, Peter put a first diver in the water who with the use of a scooter, quickly goes down on the wreck and ties up a descent line. "Go down fighting the whole way," said Peter. We quickly jumped off the boat with the hopes of grabbing the descent line and pulling ourselves down to the wreck and yes we did fight all the way down.

Once on the wreck, we kept close to the hull of the King Mitch to shelter ourselves from the current and we explored the interiors which were a marine life treasure trove.

The pelagics around the wreck were also a fantastic show. To experience the action in the blue, we found a part of the wreck to hold on to and just watched. The King Mitch is a cleaning station for eagle rays and we found a group of 20 of them, effortlessly flying over the hull in the company of barracudas.

The ship has been sliced in two and the current runs through the gap between the bow and stern. Eagle rays tend to congregate there, hovering and enjoying the gentle caress of the current.

After about fifteen minutes the show was over, and as soon as everyone had a hand on the descent line, we disconnected the line from the wreck, to float out into the open ocean. On a heavy current day, you can end up as much as a mile away from the wreck before your decompression is finished.

While waiting to be recovered by the dive boat, we relived the beauty of our dive on the King Mitch, an old minesweeper who finished its career transformed by the sea into an oasis of marine life.

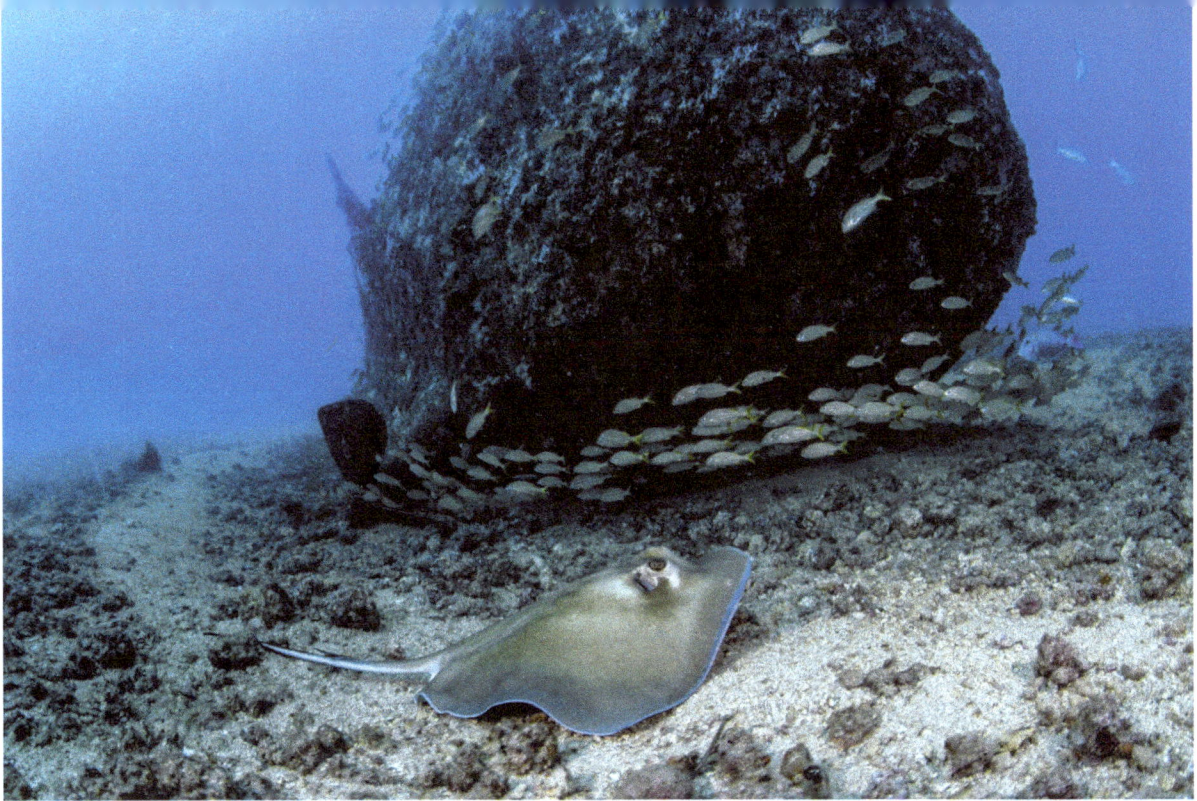

>>GRENADA
THE SAN JUAN

Swimming in perfect unison, the Atlantic spadefish perform a ballet for visiting divers.

SAN JUAN

This small 80-foot old fishing boat is a bit of a ruin. The midsection of the vessel is spread out over the ocean bottom. Only the strongest parts of the metal carcass still stands. But frankly, it is remarkable that anything at all remains of the San Juan that sank 45 years ago. Since 1975 when it sunk, the number of hurricanes that have come through Grenada is staggering. And each hurricane has taken its toll on the San Juan, even moving the wreck 1,500 feet on the sea bed.

But we weren't going diving on this shipwreck for its nautical features. We went to dive the San Juan because locally it is known as The Shark Wreck - a real magnet for shark life.

Descending the downline to the wreck, the first thing we saw were not less than 10 nurse sharks, posed on the sand near the bow. As we made a quick tour of the wreck, many of these sharks swam out on the sand, disappearing into the distance or into the inner bowels of the wreck.

At the stern of the wreck was a stingray, posed on the sand. Schools of grunts and snappers covered the mid-section and lobsters were to be found under many pieces of the wreck. From out of the blue behind the stern of the wreck, a big school of Atlantic spadefish appeared, heading to the wreck to perform a ballet for us. Each fish swam in unison, creating a unified ball of silvery life that slowly danced its way to the bow. The show of marine life on this little wreck was astonishing!

The San Juan sits 2 miles of the Atlantic cast of Grenada in 90 feet of water.

GRENADA >> THE HEMA I

The Hema 1 is one of Grenada's favorite resting place for nurse sharks, which come in large numbers.

approaching, you can share the wreck with the nurse sharks and spend some quality time observing these fascinating creatures, lying in and around the wreck.

There is a lot of current on the Hema 1. Sometimes it is impossible to get down on the wreck and even once you are down, staying on the wreck can be difficult. Back on the surface, the sea can be rough and the wind and swell picks up quickly, making the return to the boat, sometimes, a fairly acrobatic but worthwhile effort.

In 2005, Hema 1, a 170 foot Trinidadian cargo vessel had dumped a load of cement in Grenada and was on its way home to Trinidad. Seas were rough that day, as is often the case in the channel between Grenada and Trinidad. The waves started coming in and on this day, unfortunately, the bilge pumps did not work. The Captain turned the boat around, heading back to Grenada but it wasn't long before the boat filled with water and the captain needed to issue a Mayday distress signal.

The crew was saved by the Grenada Coast Guard, abandoning the boat to its fate. Hema I drifted for a while and then sank approximately 3 miles off the south coast of Grenada. The ship's new home is on a sandy bottom in 110 feet of water. She landed on her port side.

The wreck has been broken apart by severe hurricane surges and now the midship is more of a debris field. The bow is still recognizable as well as the stern and the gangway and the wheelhouse are fun parts of the wreck to visit. The cargo holds have been levelled. The panels are laid flat on the sand and form a perfect shelters for marine creatures and especially sharks.

Hema 1 is a favorite resting place for nurse sharks, which come in large numbers. Nurse sharks are unique sharks as they do not have to swim to be able to breath. They enjoy cur-

rent, that passes the water over their gills for a good supply of oxygen.

The nurse sharks are quite shy and are happier to swim out on the sand and leave the wreck when there are too many bubbles, to return as soon as divers start going up the descent line. At 110 feet in depth, our bottom time is limited to 15 minutes, while nurse sharks spend the better part of the day on the wreck. But if you are calm and take your time

>>GRENADA
THE SHAKEM

The solidified bags of cement in the hull are well organized into piles, as if they are ready to be off-loaded at the next harbour.

The Shakem ended its career as a cargo vessel transporting a very dangerous cargo between Grenada and Trinidad - bags of cement. If badly stowed, bags of cement can move and their shifting weight can dis-equilibrate the boat. And this was the fate of the Shakem.

The ship embarked on its last journey in 2001. The sea was strong and the weight of the cement had shifted. The waves began to flood into the cargo hull and the mix of water and cement in the bilge blocked the pumps. Quite quickly, the boat sunk to the bottom, within site of St George's harbour.

The freighter started a new life in 110 feet of water, lying upright on a sand bed. Being so close to the shore, it is one of the most accessible shipwrecks in Grenada but also one of the most spectacular.

After all these years, the structure of this 180 foot ship has remained intact and now is brimming with life. Due to the nutrient rich waters and the gentle current that caress the ship, gorgonians, encrusting sponges, sea fans and black coral cover many of the boat's surfaces. The stern wheelhouse, bow and propeller are some of the most colourful parts of the ship.

The remnants of the bags of cement fill the hull. The bags are solidified and are in well organized piles, as if they are ready to be off-loaded at the next harbour. The large crane, which would have lifted the bags of cement into the ship, towers over the hull. The mid-ship crane is probably the biggest highlight of the vessel, encrusted with sea fans, gorgonians and sponges.

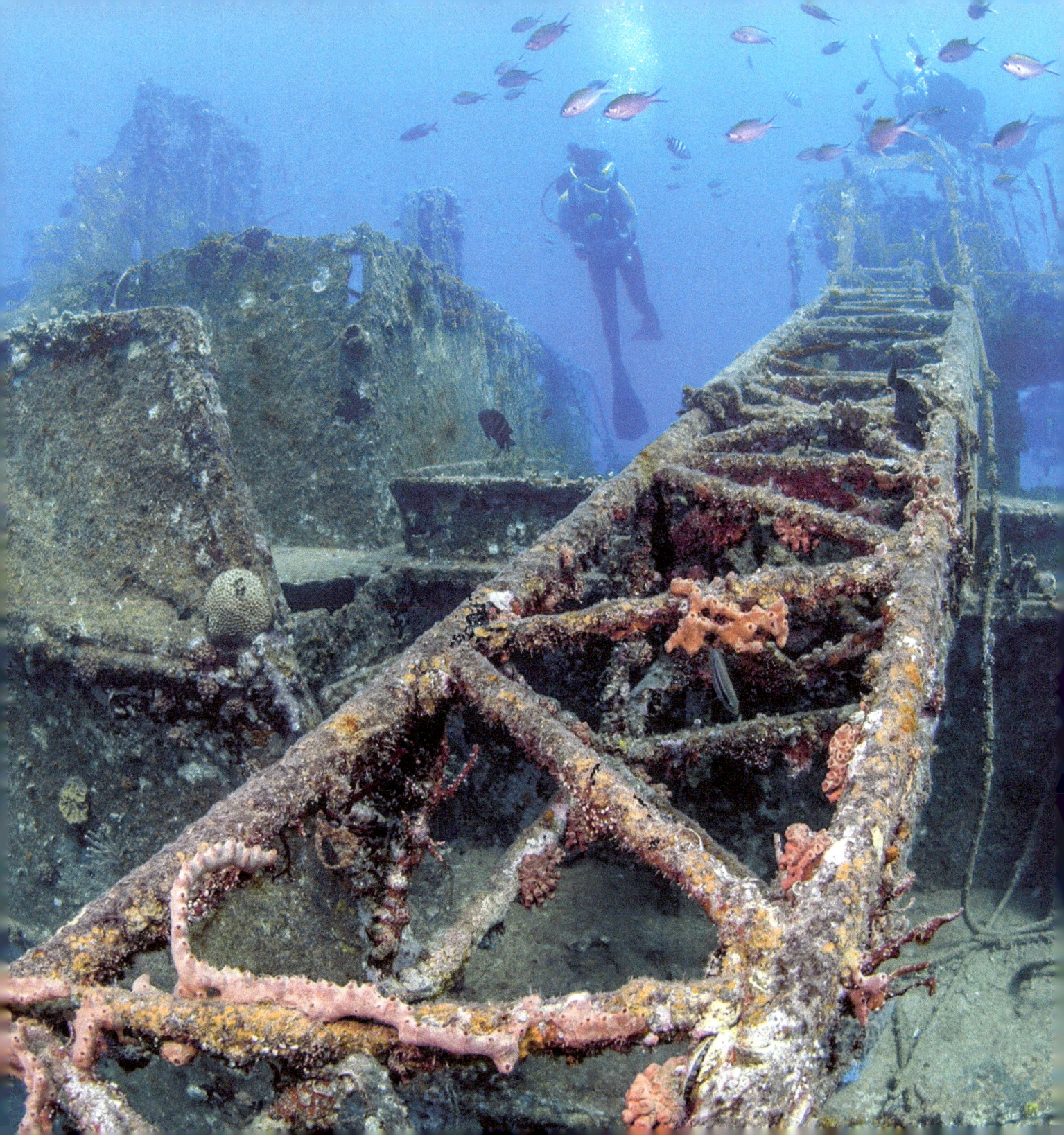

GRENADA >>VERONICA L

Well decorated with orange-cup coral and encrusting sponges, the colours are outstanding on this cute little wreck.

In 1993, while at anchor, the Veronica L, a Trinidad cargo ship, started taking on water and it was not long before she was at the bottom of the sea. The ship sank in St George's harbour, at the site of the future cruise-ship terminal. Before construction of the new terminal could began, the wreck of the Veronica L needed to be moved. Refloated and loaded onto a barge, it was hauled out to Grand Anse, where it was sunk on the reef. It landed on its keel and now has become an integral part of the reef.

This 130 foot cargo ship is a cute little wreck. Well decorated with orange-cup coral and encrusting sponges, the colours are outstanding. As it is a shallow water wreck, sitting in less than 50 feet of water, the light from the surface makes the wreck even more colourful…. yellows, oranges, pinks and purples adorn the wreck. Small schools of fish inhabit the wreck and seahorse, frog fish and eels are often spotted.

The crane, used to load the cargo into the hull, is impressive. The propeller is now gone but the lovely coral that covers the keel and rudder is worth a trip down onto the reef to take a look.

CARRIACOU >>THE TWIN TUGS

Two is company, three is a crowd, except when it comes to tugboat shipwrecks!

In Carriacou near Mabouya Island, two ocean going tugboats are sitting within a short distance of one another in less than 100 feet of water. Both are around 100 feet long.

To create artificial reefs and different dive sites, the Carriacou authorities have sunk a series of old out-of-service Grenada tugs. After being cleaned, these tugs were sunk on sandy bottoms at a depth accessible to divers.

But why tugboats? They can resist the waves and the ocean swell that break more fragile metal boats to pieces or gnaws away at wooden hulls. Also, thanks to their flat bottoms, tugboats are stable on the ocean floor and remain upright and vertical, giving the diver a sense that the underwater tug is ready to set sail.

The Westsider was sunk in 2004 and The Boris was sunk 3 years later in 2007. Their metallic structures have become decorated with corals, sponges and gorgonians. On the bridge and in the holds, schools of small fish have concentrated which in turn, has attracted predatory barracudas and sharks to the bridge. As with many sites in Grenada and Carriacou, the current can sometimes be strong, which adds to the diversity of life that you can see on the wreck.

In 2018 the 130 foot tugboat called the Mammoth Troll was also sunk in the waters close to the Twin Tugs. Penetration is possible into various sections of the vessel, and there is a great swim-through running the length of the superstructure.

>>CARRIACOU
THE ROSE

A magnet for southern stingrays

The Rose is a 56 foot sail boat which sunk in 2003 in Tyrell Bay off the island of Carriacou. The wreck is lying in 70 feet of water on a sandy bottom with sea grass all around. The Rose is often visited by southern stingrays. Inside the wreck, groupers and schooling snappers and grunts shelter.

>>MUSTIQUE
THE SS ANTILLES

Why the Captain of the SS Antilles decided to sail into the narrow, shallow strait is still not known.

The French cruise ship, the SS Antilles was built in 1952 and began sailing the waters of the Caribbean for the French Line in the 1960s.

In 1971, the SS Antilles struck a reef near the island of Mustique in the Grenadines while attempting to navigate a bay. Why the Captain of the SS Antilles decided to sail into the narrow, shallow strait between The Pillories is still not known. Some believe the Captain wanted to show his passengers the beaches of Mustique that Princess Margaret frequented with her lover. As the story goes, the curious on deck turned their binoculars towards Mustique, hoping to catch a glimpse.

But suddenly the liner stopped with a crash. When the ship hit the rocks, passengers fell one on top of each other and the liner was trapped in a coral reef. The fuel tank of the Antilles ruptured and caught on fire, forcing 690 people to abandon the burning ship. The British luxury liner Queen Elizabeth 2 picked up passengers and crew members who had fled the Antilles in lifeboats.

The Antilles' burnt-out hull could not be freed from the reef and the ship lay there for several months before it broke in two. Years later, the Antilles, an eyesore to many Mustique residents, still sat above the waterline. Eventually, following several salvaging operations as well as attempts to move the wreck, the metallic structure collapsed and the charred carcass disappeared under the surface… but just under the surface. It is still, till this day, a navigational obstacle.

Diving on this shallow water wreck is not easy. The waves and surge push you onto sharp, rusty pieces of the wreck that are only 5 feet from the surface. And the current is strong. The bow of the ship rises to 10 feet below the surface with its winches encrusted with colourful corals and sea fans. The mammoth anchor chain and windlass rest on the deck. The midsection of the boat is a bit of a debris field as it has collapsed. The broilers remain strong and intact. But by far the most spectacular part of the wreck is the stern section with its huge propellers. It is when we see the propellers that we realize the amplitude of this wreck. Lying on the bottom, the propellers are attached to the keel by their long metal shafts.

>>BEQUIA
RICK'S H

The southern tip of Bequia is a navigational trap for those in a hurry to arrive at Admiralty Bay.

At the southern tip of Bequia in the Grenadines is an enormous natural arch through which the moon can be seen. The place is rightfully called Moonhole. In the 60s, an American couple came to Bequia, acquired the tip of the island and built their home under Moonhole. They created an architectural wonder built into the landscape, using natural stone and whale bones, which they found on the beach. Their quirky home blurred the line between indoor and outdoor space. Later they would build 17 mores homes and create a community of like minded people.

Sailing from Martinique to Grenada we stopped for the night in Bequia. At a local bar, we were told about a wreck just off Moonhole and the next morning we set off to find it. Our trip out to Moonhole was spectacular. The dramatic shoreline in itself was worth the trip. A mooring buoy on Moonhole reef was our entry point into the water. Rick's H is down on a sand bed past the reef in 130 feet of water. A 240-foot container ship, it's presence in the underwater landscape is impressive.

How did the wreck end up there? This corner of Bequia is a natural shipwreck maker. Cutting the corner short on the turn into Admiralty Bay could easily land you on the reef.

>>MARTINIQUE
THE TAMAYA

In 1902, the eruption of Mount Pelée devastated the city of Saint-Pierre in Martinique. With 33,000 deaths, this volcanic disaster is one of the most deadly in the history of mankind. All the ships at anchor in the bay sunk, creating a shipwreck graveyard at the bottom of the sea. The last to be discovered was the mysterious Tamaya.

On the morning of May 8, 1902, the eruption of the volcano surprised the ships at anchor in the harbor. For several months already, Mont Pelée, which overlooks the bay of Saint-Pierre, was showing its ill-humor. Dull rumblings, noises and sulphurous plumes of vapor disturbed the inhabitants, and the roofs of the town of Saint-Pierre were covered with gray ash. But the commanders of the ships could not imagine the cataclysm that was to strike them at sea.

At eight o'clock in the morning, a series of thunderclaps shook Saint-Pierre. From the flanks of the volcano emerged a fiery cloud, which first rose in the atmosphere, then rolled down the slopes of Mont Pelée. Aboard the ships, the sailors saw the clouds swirling, before falling onto the small town, covering it with a mantle of incandescent ashes. A few minutes later, the ships were surrounded in a tornado of fire. Sails of cotton, rigs of hemp, barrels of rum, of sugar and of molasses burnt first. The vessels, restrained by their anchors, could not escape. The "Roddam", a steamer, was the only boat that managed to cut its line and escape, reaching the open sea and the island of St Lucia. A few hours later, only smoldering wrecks remained in the bay. On board, burnt survivors died agonizing deaths, before the ships sank into oblivion.

It was not until 1960 that the wrecks were spotted by fishermen and explored by the first Martinican divers. Since that time, the site has become a world renowned wreck diving zone. Dozens of sailboats, steamers and tugboats have been discovered and identified by local divers.

The bay was believed to be fully documented by 1980. In that year, Jacques Cousteau's team filmed and photographed the wrecks. Based on a picture taken on the eve of the eruption, there was no trouble finding the wrecks, practically at the same place as they were anchored. Yet a cable boat, the Grappler, was not where they had expected to find it. The Grappler was a great ship that, according to the rumors of the time, was carrying a treasure.

In 1983, a French National Navy boat called "L'entrecastreau", equipped with a magnetometer started searching the bay of Saint Pierre. On the edge of the drop off, they registered a mysterious deep-water echo that would bring back to life the legend of a treasure in the bay of Saint-Pierre, dating back to the

1900s. Was the echo taken by the French navy that of the Grappler - was the wreck finally found?

I, Dominique Serafini, had the privilege of being able to be one of the very first dives on this wreck, captured by the magnetometer. It remains engraved in my memory as one of the most impressive dives of my life. I descended in the blue along the buoy-line that marked the position of the echo. I descended, crossing the twilight zone of about 235 feet. The dark, jagged silhouette of a long hull lying on star-

board, hanging on the edge of a rocky ridge overlooking a vertiginous cliff, appeared to me. No doubt, blown by the tornado of fire, this sailboat had broken its moorings, drifted, and then sunk out of the anchorage zone. Its iron hull was miraculously hanging at the edge of the fall off - a position so inconceivable that the wreckage had eluded all research on the shipwrecks done in the bay to date.

I was struck, and am to this day, by the beauty of the shipwreck.

On my first dive, I quickly drew an overall view of the ship. Once back on shore, I filed a public declaration of the wreck and published the sketch in France Antilles. This triggered a bit of a riot in the Martinique dive community and launched a race to identify the wreck and perhaps find the treasure.

Anyway, the wreck was not the Grappler, but the Nantes three-masted sailboat, the "Tamaya" and the crazy treasure race came to an end. After a decree of the Attorney General of Martinique prohibiting the organization of sport dives on this deep wreck, the calm returned to Saint-Pierre.

This wreck was a treasure. This treasure that had nothing to do with the classic chest filled with jewelry and currency. It was a beautiful and ominous wreck but there is more. The Tamaya's treasure was discovered by François Villecart. A savvy businessman, he launched a rather crazy project: an underwater submarine called Mobilis that visited the wrecks of Saint-Pierre, and most notably, the Tamaya. The Mobilis was a superb submersible built in Germany by the firm Bruker, designed to carry 50 passengers up to 100 meters. At first skeptical and incredulous, the political leaders of Saint-Pierre were seduced by this exceptional project. Several economic partners financed the operation, and the submarine began its trips.

Comfortably seated in front of the circular portholes, tourists were able to discover the main wrecks of the bay of Saint-Pierre during a dive of about an hour: the "Diamond", the "Teresa Lovigo", the "Clementina", The "Roraima", a 300 foot long steamship, and most importantly, the "Tamaya" at a depth of 285 feet.

The carcasses of the wrecks, burnt by the eruption, took nearly a century to become beautiful underwater oasis.

After just 10 years of submarines and divers, the wrecks were quickly turning back into carcasses. In summer months, the water visibility was poor enough that seeing the wrecks from the submarine was almost impossible. As a result, the submarine approached the wrecks often too closely. These historic shipwrecks were beginning to be damaged and complaints were filed against the submarine - and against the dive shops, who often threw their anchors on the wrecks. As a result, the Mobilis submarine operation was eventually stopped and the Tamaya is once again, a deep wreck, not frequently visited and frozen in time, 285 feet under the sea.

75

MARTINIQUE >>THE RORAIMA

Even though the lionfish have replaced the sailors and
passengers, their phantoms still haunt this dramatic wreck
that sank in 1902.

In the bay of Saint-Pierre, there is one
wreck that captures the imagination of divers - the Titanic of Martinique, The Roraima.
At 165 feet, its iron hull is planted on a bed
of grey mud. Its large bow stands proud
and vertically on the bottom. A dive on the
Roraima, is to relive a dramatic historic event.

The sailors and the passengers aboard the
boat in May 1902 would have been worried
about hurricanes and storms but never would
they have imagined being hit by such a cataclysm, sprung from the bowels of the earth.

The Roraima was a mixed cargo vessel,
owned by the Quebec Line. It left Montreal,
sailed to New York, on to Bermuda, Barbados
and finally, it made a stop in Martinique in the

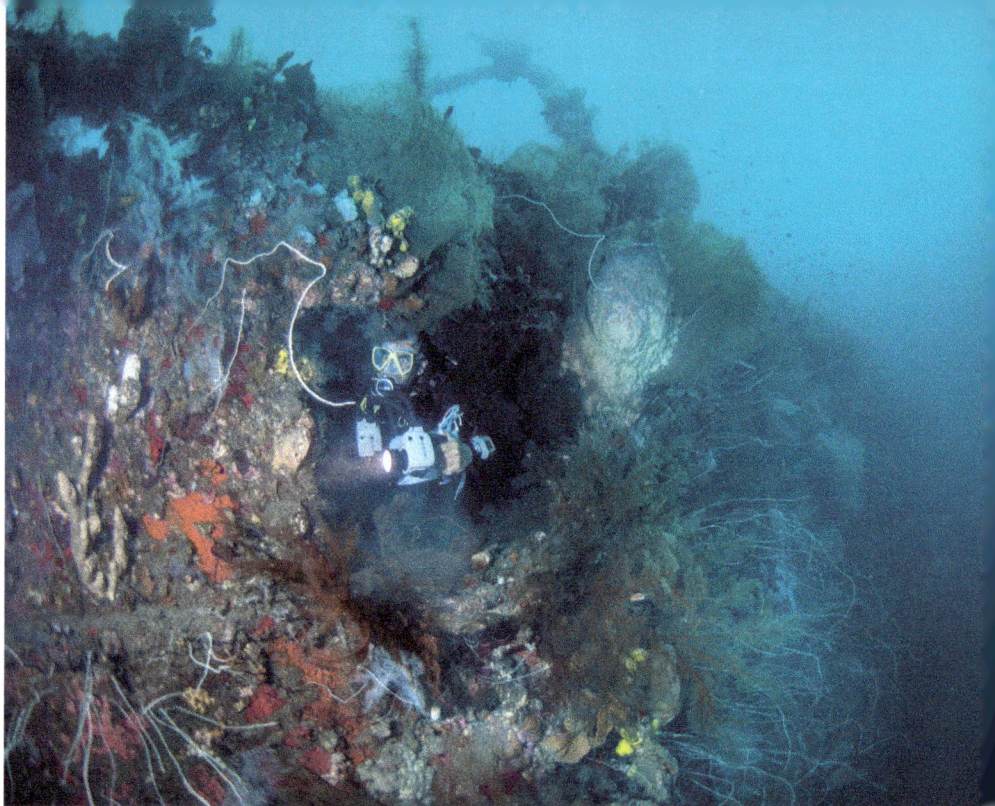
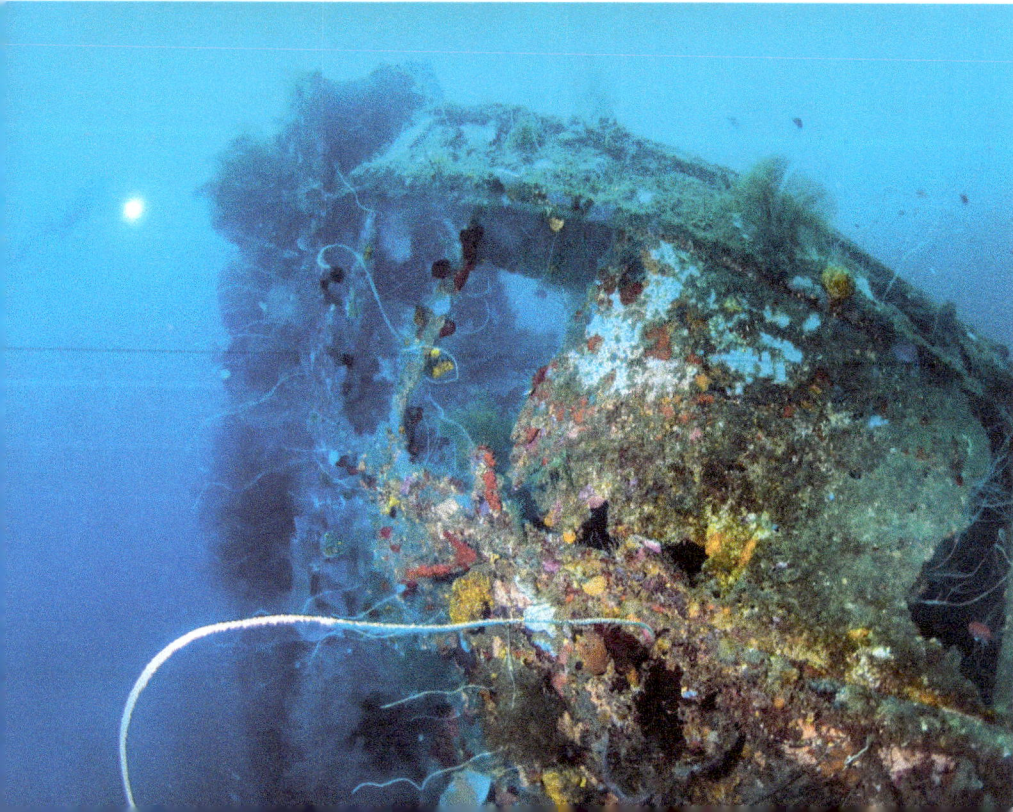

bay of Saint-Pierre. After such a long journey, the passengers were happy to make a stop in a harbour, known as the little Paris of the Antilles. Unfortunately, this stop would be their last one - a stop in hell!

On the morning of May 8, 1902, the passengers were on the deck of the mixed cargo vessel, looking at a spectacular site. Mont Pelée, which dominated the town of Saint-Pierre was covered with clouds. The sky was blue but there were grey clouds. Many passengers took photos, some were looking through binoculars.

The officers of the Roraima knew that the volcano had been active for over a month but the port authorities had assured them that the volcano spitted ashes and sulphur but there was nothing to worry about. On the Roraima, the officers thought they were out of the range of danger. The fast modern steam engines would permit them to escape rapidly if there was a danger and the lava hit the sea.

The cathedral bells rang 8am. Mont Pelée opened

79

THE RORAIMA
SAINT PIERRE - MARTINIQUE

The Forecastle

Port Side Tunnel

The Chimney

Access to the Galley

The Boilers

The Bow

The Forecastle

The Stern Hull

Starboard Gangway

Machine Room Window

A Starboard Davit

Cargo Hull

The Stern Deck

up and let loose a fiery cloud - a whirlwind of flames and ashes rose in the sky like a giant dragon. In a few seconds, the whirlwind descended on the town of Saint-Pierre. The passengers of the Roraima look on with horror as the town disappeared under a black shroud.

Boats in the bay exploded in a burst of fire. Sailors on the deck of the Roraima ran in all directions as the captain tried to set sail. But the boat was struck by a tsunami of fire and all are killed by the burning gas. The captain, then blinded, fell into the sea, into the bubbling water. A few on board the Roraima, hidden from the burning cloud, managed to survive

and remained on board the smoking carcass of the boat until rescued days later.

115 years later, the sea has changed the wreck of the Roraima. It has put a "carnival" mask of colour on the wreck. Coral and sponges cover the burnt out hull of the ship and dissimulate the scars of the eruption.

Whenever I go into the engine room, or swim down the corridors or on the bridge of the Roraima, I still feel the presence of the victims of this eruption. Even though the lionfish have replaced the sailors and passengers, their phantoms still haunt this dramatic wreck.

>>MARTINIQUE
THE NAHOON

Sunk with its three masts in place, the Nahoon was a surreal spectacle! It's like the Nahoon had continued it's sail-worthy journey into another world.

In the north of Martinique are the wonderful wrecks of The Roraima and The Tamaya. Both are part of the shipwreck grave-yard of the bay of St-Pierre, a result of the volcanic explosion of 1902. But in the south of the island of Martinique, where divers flock in greater numbers to see the beautiful reef of Diamond Rock, shipwrecks are a rarity.

It was the year 1993. An old sailboat called The Nahoon was rusting away gently in the bay of Fort de France. This boat had already built fortunes for different owners – it was a lighthouse boat, a charter boat, a floating restaurant and a night-club. It had been passed from owner to owner and now it was aban-doned, likely to finish its life as an old piece of rusty metal on the shore, scavenged by scrap collectors.

A visionary dive club saw the beauty of this vessel as a ship-wreck and was willing to offer The Nahoon a peaceful end to its long career, far from the people who had abandoned it in the bay.

A beautiful morning in 1992, the Nahoon, after being

cleaned of environmental debris and its hulls emptied, was towed in what was much like a funeral procession towards Cap Salomon, where the sailboat would be sunk onto a white sand bottom. Close to the shore, in 130 feet of water, the Nahoon sank.

Fish immediately took refuge in the wreck and divers flocked to see this beautiful wreck. Upright with two of the three masts and rigging in place, it is a wonderful and surreal sight! It appears like the Nahoon is continuing it's sail-worthy journey into another world.

A visit to the Nahoon is well worth it - schools of silvery barracudas and jacks hover between the masts above the wreck and colourful reef fish swim in and around the metal structure. 25 years later, sponges and corals decorate the hull of the boat with yellow, orange, red and purple. It's a colourful wreck with a magical look to it.

The large steering wheel on the deck evokes your imagination. You can see yourself at the helm, steering the boat through a terrible storm.

The last time we were on the wreck, there was only one mast left. Over time, the fishermen have caught their lines in the boat's rigging, the waves and storms have beaten the hull and divers, sadly, have contributed to the Nahoon's inevitable wear and tear.

Let yourself be carried by the current far in front of the wreck. Take your time and slowly approach the wreck along the bottom. The wreck will gradually come into view and that is a really striking vision! The Nahoon appears to be sailing towards you from out of the fog, heading off for its last and arguably its finest cruise.

>>NEVIS
THE CHRISTENA

On August 1, 1970 Nevis was changed forever, when most people from the island lost a loved-one in this tragic inter-island ferry disaster.

MV Christena was a 160-foot, government-owned and operated ferry boat, which worked the 12-mile route between St. Kitts, and Nevis.

The passenger ferryboat sank in the Narrows–a thin strait between the islands–on August 1, 1970 when the captain failed to close the vessel's watertight doors. Workmen had been repairing the propeller shaft below decks and they assumed the captain would make a final check before departing St. Kitts for Nevis.

Designed to carry 180 passengers, the boat was overloaded with over 300 happy people heading home to Nevis from an Emancipation Day holiday celebration. Not long out of port, the ferryboat started to capsize and the captain turned his vessel sharply toward shore in an attempt to run it aground. But the bulky, top-heavy boat capsized quickly. Fishing boats and pleasure craft came to the rescue, but only 91 people survived, and the great majority of those were people that had to be rescued.

The Christena was a converted river boat built in New Orleans to which a steel

superstructure had been added. It had two passenger decks, the lower one enclosed. The ferry was unstable because ballast had been removed to make it ride higher in the water and keep the sea from washing over the decks. Most of the survivors were on the open upper deck.

After the ferry boat sank, numerous injured people were in the water, and the blood attracted the sharks. Of the 233 casualties, 57 bodies were retrieved and identified; 66 bodies were retrieved but were unidentifiable. A number of bodies were trapped inside the sunken wreckage, and these bodies were left in place

The Christena is a protected marine memorial park that respects those who were lost in the disaster.

With the permission of the marine park, we visited the wreck of the Christena. Visiting the wreck was a very sobering experience and one that we did not take lightly. Sitting upright in the sand at 70 feet, the wreck looks like a ghost of its former self. Dense marine growth covers the boat, enhanced by small lacy hydroids. Much of the structure of the ferry is still intact, leaving your imagination to recreate the events of its' final journey. We visited both the engine compartments and the passenger areas. The interior of the ferry was very grim. Inside the wreck, skulls and skeletal remains of those who had been trapped inside lay along side bottles of whatever was consumed the day it went down.

To honour the memory of those lost in this tragic sinking, divers from St. Kitts and Nevis conduct a yearly memorial dive.

>>ANEGADA
THE MS ROCUS

Diving on this eerie underwater ossuary is like a walk through the catacombs of Paris.

Anegada is known for miles of white sand beaches and the 18-mile-long Horseshoe Reef, one of the largest barrier coral reefs in the Caribbean. The reef extends into one of the major trading routes of the Caribbean, making navigation in Anegada's waters difficult.

There are over 300 shipwrecks in Horseshoe Reef with most of them happening between 1654 and 1899. All that remains of these wooden ships are piles of ballast stones and cannons. These wrecks include the wreck of the famous HMS Astrea which sunk in 1808. The Astrea was a 32-gun British boat that saw action in the American War of Independence. Modern steel hulled boats wrecks are more visible on the reef. We visited one such wreck - this one with a real sinister feel to it!

The wreck of the Rocus, a 380-foot steel steamship that sank in 1929 is on the southern tip of Horseshoe Reef. Not many people visit this wreck as it is quite difficult to find. The barrier reef is a shallow labyrinth and the remains of the wreck are to be found somewhere within. You swim a little to the south, a little to the north, looking for familiar landmarks but landmarks are hard to find and you turn in circles. The current, strong in places, makes the job of finding the wreck even harder.

The Rocus was taking its cargo from Trinidad to Baltimore when it hit the reef. But this was not any kind of cargo. The Rocus was carrying cow bones which would be ground up into bone meal and used as fertilizer. Her cargo of bones is now strewn along the reef among shallow water coral and ship parts. The wreck has been rightfully renamed The Bone Wreck. This ossuary contributes to a macabre feeling when diving the wreck, much like walking through

the catacombs of Paris. On the nearby Cow Wreck Beach, instead of finding sea glass or shells, you'll uncover cow bones that have washed ashore.

The stern of the wreck lies in about 40-feet of water with the bow in shallower water, broken up from the numerous hurricanes that have passed through Anegada. The engine, large boilers and winches are still recognizable.

The most iconic element of the ship is the enormous rudder, covered with orange cup and fire coral. As the precious propeller is missing, there is a nice swim through between the rudder and the keel.

>>ANEGADA
THE PARAMATTA

A side-wheel steamship is a rare treat, especially placed right in the heart of a living and colourful reef.

The Paramatta was a British Royal Mail Line side-wheel steamship. In 1859, The Paramatta sailed its maiden voyage from Southampton (England) to Cartagena de Indias (Colombia) via Tortola with 180 people on board and a cargo of coal. But this would be the only voyage that the Paramatta would make.

After leaving England and crossing the Atlantic without a problem the Captain of the Paramatta thought he had almost reached the end of his first cross-ing. He needed to pass through Anegada's channel to reach the port of Tortola, anchor and disembark some of his passengers. In the 1800s, navigational tools were not like today. A sextant was used for navigation, using the sun to calculate your relative position. Figuring out your longitude and latitude was a difficult calculation and not very precise. And maps of the time were inaccurate. An error of a few miles could result in a fatal end to your voyage.

Due to a navigational error, apparently caused by compass error from the metal hull, the Paramatta hit Horseshoe reef, Anegada Island's fringing coral reef and ran aground. The captain of the Paramatta, believing he was in a channel of deep water was going full speed when he realized his mistake. Too late to reverse, the Paramatta hit the reef and soon would become the reef's prisoner. The stranded boat became motionless.

On June 30th, 1859, everyone on board - passengers and crew - were disembarked and the boat was emptied of its cargo. For almost a month, a salvage mission was attempted, but finally The Paramatta could not be re-floated and was abandoned to her destiny.

For years, her hull remained visible as a signal on the horizon to warn other boats of the dangers of Horseshoe Reef. Eventually, the metal shell, eaten away by salt, collapsed and disappeared under the surface.

If you are passionate about historic shipwrecks, an expedition to the Paramatta is really worthwhile. Among all the wrecks of the Caribbean, the Paramatta is one of the most spectacular ones. A side-wheel steamship is a rare treat, especially placed right in the heart of a living and colourful reef.

To visit this wreck, we chose a calm day with little wind or swell and we had the GPS point, essential for finding this wreck. The final approach to the wreck we did with our dinghy, zig-zagging between very shallow patches of coral. We feared breaking our propeller on the reef, which would have been a catastrophe as Anegada is far away from the repair shop in Tortola!

Once in the water, we carefully slid through a labyrinth of coral claws that protect this living fortress. In the distance, we saw a vertical form, amongst the sea fans and elkhorn coral. The stern of the Paramatta stands upright. It's the only part of the wreck that has resisted the sea and the storms. As we got closer, we saw a school of barracudas hover in the blue, seemingly guarding the carcass. The metal ribs of the hull, covered by encrusting coral, are still holding. Dominique swam between the bars to get a closer look what else is left of the steamship. Most of the boat's metallic hull has been digested by the sea and the two paddle wheels unfortunately are broken up. Over the years, the wreck has merged with the reef to become part of the coral garden. Quite beautifully, the sea has transformed the Paramatta into a chaotic and mysterious relic of the past - a real dream wreck!

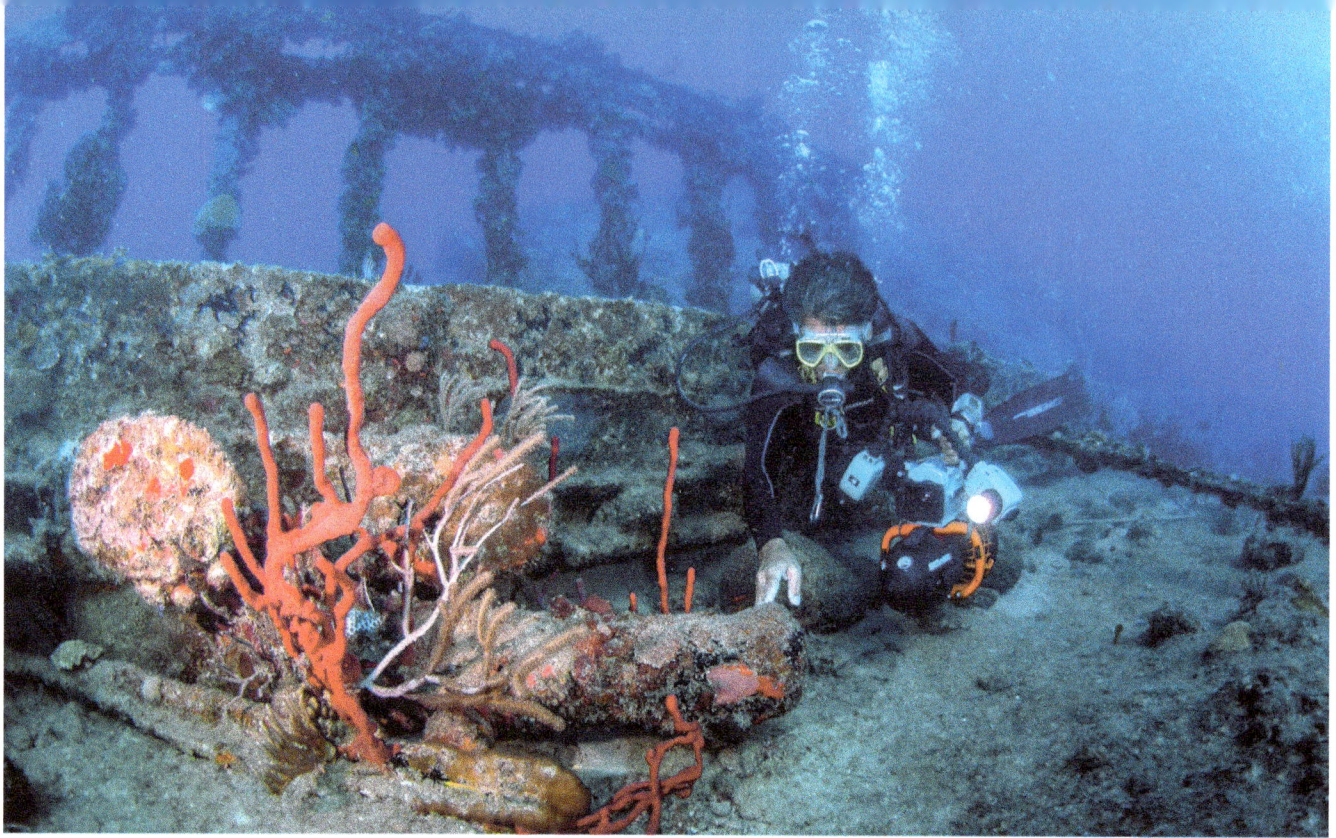

TORTOLA >>THE RMS RHONE

The British Virgin Islands is a popular tourist area for the wealthy. Luxury villas on the islands and at sea, sailboats gliding between the islands on turquoise water. But dreams can turn into nightmares when a hurricane sweeps through the islands, as did on the night in 1867 when The Rhone sunk.

Hurricane Irma struck the Virgin Islands in September 2017 with gusts of wind at 200 kilometres/hour. Homes, hotels and marinas flew away and boats were submerged, broken and sunk. Irma was a terrible surprise for the residents of these islands who thought they were safe and had forgotten the hurricane that had hit this area 150 years ago and caused a serious maritime tragedy. In 1867, as a result of a ferocious hurricane, the RMS Rhone sunk.

The Rhone was built in 1863 and put into service for The Royal Mail Steam Packet Com-

pany (RMSP), delivering mail, passengers and cargo on scheduled routes between Southampton England, The Caribbean and Brazil. The Rhone travelled the Brazilian route and later to the Caribbean.

The Rhone was a sail-steamer. It was one of the first great sailing ships with a fast engine, a bronze propeller and two masts. It was a luxurious vessel with fine lines and a marvel of technology. Furthermore, it had weathered many storms and was reputed unsinkable, like the Titanic.

October 19, 1867, The Rhone was anchored in Great Harbour, Peter Island, a sheltered and relatively calm mooring. Captain Woolley was delivering his cargo of precious wood and unloading his passengers when he noticed that the pressure of his barometer was falling rapidly. Black clouds barred the horizon and there was no wind. The atmosphere had become oppressive.

The hurricane season was over but as a precaution Woolley decided to hasten his departure before the possible arrival of a hurri-

cane. He believed it more prudent to leave his anchorage so as not to be surprised in the bay. He even embarked on board passengers from another boat which was not as sea-worthy as the Rhone.

To prevent the passengers from being injured or swept away by the waves at sea, Woolley ordered the cabins locked and the passengers tied to their beds. The Rhone was ready to sail but the anchor was stuck, wrapped around a coral head. Time was ticking and the storm progressing so the Captain decided to cut the chain of the anchor. Confident in the power of his engine, he chose to take a short-cut through the narrow passage between Salt Island and Dead Chest Island, a risky manoeuvre. Unfortunately, the hurricane swells shifted and the boat was thrown directly onto the tip of Black Rock Point. On contact, the ship broke into two and the steam engine explod-

The Rhone was built in 1863 and commissioned for the Royal Mail Steam Packet Company (RMSP), delivering mail and passengers.

ed and the Captain disappeared overboard. The panicked crew tried to launch boats in the raging sea and in their cabins the passengers screamed in terror.

The next morning, when the sea calmed, the inhabitants of Salt Island found dozens of passengers stranded on the rocks and 123 corpses strewn on the beach. The bodies of these 123 victims where later buried on Salt Island and today, we can still see the wooden crosses planted among the stones.

The mast of the Rhone was visible from the surface and the stern of the wreck sat shallow 30 feet of water. According to historical accounts, part of the cargo carried by the Rhone was gold coins. Divers were apparently hired to salvage the ship's cargo.

In the 70s, the movie The Deep was shot on the Rhone with actress Jacqueline Bisset and a giant moray eel, hidden in the wreck, ready to devour the divers. This movie popularized the Rhone and turned this wreck into a famous dive site that has attracted hundreds of divers each year.

Treasure hunters were attracted to the Rhone, hoping to find gold coins that were not found in the initial salvage. It seems that from time to time, divers are finding treasures on the wreck - dishes, cutlery, bottles and even some gold coins. After a new hurricane upsets a wreck, moving pieces of the hull or rocks, ob-

jects buried in the sand move to the surface and divers sometimes find beautiful surprises.

On our dives on the wreck, we found the best treasure of all - witnessing and photographing this fantastic historic shipwreck! The wreck of the Rhone is located within a marine reserve and so it's resident groupers, snappers, moray eels and lobsters are protected on this artificial reef.

In the 1950s, the wreck was judged a navigational hazard and the Royal Navy dynamited the stern section of the Rhone. Now the wreck's bow and stern section are spread apart and takes two separate dives to see the complete wreck.

The bow, the most intact part of the wreck, is sitting in deeper water at 80 feet. The metal shell of the wreck is encrusted with colourful coral and sponges. Rigging dead-eyes, laden with coral, adorn the edges of the hull. The bowsprit of the ship proudly points forward. The hatch in the bow leads to a dark and mysterious corridor covered by orange cup coral. Caribbean spiny lobsters populate the wreck. The mast and the crows nest lie on the sand and provide a home for a large school of snappers.

The mid-section has metal beams still standing, like Greek columns in the Parthenon. A cannon lie at the base of the columns.

A second shallow dive on the stern of the Rhone is also worth while. In just 30 feet of water, the stern has a wonderful propeller with 3 huge bronze blades and a beautiful swim through. And why not a third night dive on the wreck…. beautiful and mysterious!

93

>>TORTOLA
CHIKUZEN

Ironically, schools of fish now seek shelter in this ship that once served as a refrigerator vessel for the fishing industry.

The Chikuzen was a 240 foot Korean refrigerator vessel based in St. Maarten used at dock to service big Korean fishing fleets. It was early in 1981 when a hurricane was approaching St. Maarten. The government told the owners to move the decrepit ship so it wouldn't sink in the harbour or damage the docks.

The owners thought this would be a good chance to get rid of the ship once and for all. The owners set the Chikuzen on fire and sent it adrift, hoping it would sink just offshore. The smouldering vessel went adrift and ended up in the British Virgin Islands, close to Tortola, where it finally sunk. The wreck now serves a new purpose. Resting in 75 feet of water far from any reef, the Chikuzen is a magnet for marine life like an oasis in the desert.

Diving the Chikuzen is not always possible because of its exposed location and big swells but this is a wonderful dive if the conditions are right. Large pelagic fish, sharks and rays congregate around the wreck and in the inside, large schools of reef fish seek shelter.

We began our dive on the Chikuzen, greeted by hundreds, if not thousands of barracuda, hanging around the downline in 20 feet of water. A fantastic spectacle but we were there to see the Chikuzen so we continued our journey to the bottom of the sea.

We were blessed with good visibility and on our descent, we could see the entire 240 foot wreck. At the stern of the Chikuzen were some unusual pelagics on the sand - a pair of cobias. That was the first time and the last time I've seen these bizarre looking fish.

With all our noisy bubbles, they quickly disappeared into the blue.

The ship is on its port side with the starboard rail reaching up to about 50 feet. Most of the ship is intact, with three large cargo holds that can be entered through open hatches. We visited each hull, and had nice surprises in each one. In the first we found a turtle sleeping. Once awake, the turtle swam towards the surface for a breath of air. In another hull, schools of grunts and snappers swam between the refrigerator piping. Ironically, small fish now seek shelter in a ship that once served as a refrigerator vessel for the fishing industry. In the last hull, was a Goliath grouper - surely a permanent resident of the wreck for the large supply of schooling fish. Back outside the wreck, a huge stingray buried in the sand gracefully swam up and over the Chikuzen in a grand finale.

TORTOLA >>THE FEARLESS

A night dive on the sister ship of the Calypso brings back haunting memories.

The wreck of The Fearless is a half hour boat ride from Tortola in the British Virgin Islands. A wooden hulled mine-sweeper, the Fearless is the sister-ship of Jacques Yves Cousteau's Calypso. With that in mind, we decided to visit this wreck so that Dominique could relive some memories of his past, when he worked on board the Calypso. For Dominique, his days working with Cousteau were the pinnacle of his professional career.

Built in 1942 in Seattle, the Calypso was an old boat from the Second World War. In 1950 after the war it was bought by the Guinness beer family and given as a gift to Cousteau. For close to 50 years, the boat was lovingly patched together by the mechanics and the rest of the Cousteau team. Calypso managed to survive a gruelling trip to the Antarctic and many hurricanes and storms but finally sunk in the Singapore harbour.

We decided to do a night dive on the Fearless. Dominique's idea was to bring back memories, visiting his cabin and some familiar corners of the mine-sweeper.

The last imagined voyage of Calypso to the bottom of the sea.

The wreck sits upright on the sand in 80 feet of water. It appeared out of the blackness like a haunted castle. Its wooden structure was quite rotten and the inside of the wreck felt very unsafe. A barracuda patrolled the deck of this phantom wreck. We surfaced from our dive unsure whether this wreck is a dream or a nightmare.

Another nearby wreck at a dive site called Coral Gardens is a small airplane which has become a magnet for sea life. It was an opportunity to lighten things up with some underwater antics in the cockpit.

>>ST THOMAS
USS LST-467

Orange cup coral decorate the Caribbean's most colourful, coral encrusted wreck.

Built in 1942, The USS LST-467 was a United States Navy LST-1-class tank landing ship used in the Asiatic-Pacific Theatre during World War II. As with many of her class, the ship was never named. Instead, the ship was referred to by its hull designation.

Landing Ship, Tank (LST), or tank landing ship, is the naval designation for ships first developed during World War II to support amphibious operations by carrying tanks, vehicles, cargo, and landing troops directly onto shore with no docks or piers. This enabled amphibious assaults on almost any beach. The bow of the LST had a large door that would open with a ramp for unloading the vehicles. The LST had a special flat keel that allowed the ship to be beached and stay upright. The twin propellers and rudders had protection from grounding.

LST-467 earned eight battle stars and the Navy Unit Commendation for World War II service and was credited with shooting down five enemy planes.

Following the war, LST-467 returned to the United States,

Some of the most spectacular highlights of the wreck were the large coral encrusted orange and yellow cargo crane, the impressive propeller half buried in the sand, the wheelhouse, the galley and the deck hardware and railings.

was decommissioned and refitted as a cargo ship. Over the years, the freighter was bought and sold several times, including a stint in Canada hauling logs. The last owner was the West Indies Trading company that bought the ship in 1973. They renamed the ship WIT Shoal II and it was used as an inter-island freighter in the Caribbean. In 1984, Tropical Storm Klaus created havoc in the US Virgin Islands and the WIT Shoal sank just off Charlotte Amalie. The ship's career as a freighter was over. The owners patched, raised and sold the ship for scrap in Puerto Rico. However while being towed to Puerto Rico, one of the hull patches broke loose and the tow lines had to be cut. The WIT Shoal sank 2 miles south off of St Thomas.

The whereabouts of the LST-467 was unknown to the general public for years but eventually, St. Thomas divers found it.

The ship is a large 400-foot cargo shipwreck sitting upright on a featureless sand plane, 90 feet below the surface. Towering 70 feet out of the sand from keel to wheelhouse, it has five decks - from the first level engine room to the Captain's control room. The immensity of the wreck is overwhelming. We were in awe when we got our first glimpse of the wreck.

A ripping current surrounded the wreck. Bathed by currents, this wreck is the most colourful wrecks of the Caribbean. Coated with Tubastraea or Orange Cup Coral, it is an un-

derwater painting. A school of horse-eyed jacks floated effortlessly in the current at the stern of the wreck. We however, needed to duck into the wheelhouse regularly to recover from the work of staying abreast with the jacks.

The wreck is a virtual magnet for marine life and many fish have taken up residence in this steel reef. Barracudas hung out on the deck and we saw a few turtles swimming around the superstructure. Large Southern stingrays rest on the deck and can be seen in the sand surrounding the shell of the ship. The shadowed recesses of the hold are home to Goliath grouper and reef sharks make occasional patrols of the area. The life on the wreck was astonishing.

Some of the most spectacular highlights of the wreck were the large coral encrusted orange and yellow cargo crane, the impressive propeller half buried in the sand, the wheelhouse, the galley and the deck hardware and railings. But with only a few dives on this wreck, we still have so much more to discover.

There is a great community interest in this wreck. There have been a couple of reunions organized for soldiers who served on the ship during the Second World War and efforts are underway to have LST-467 declared a historical site.

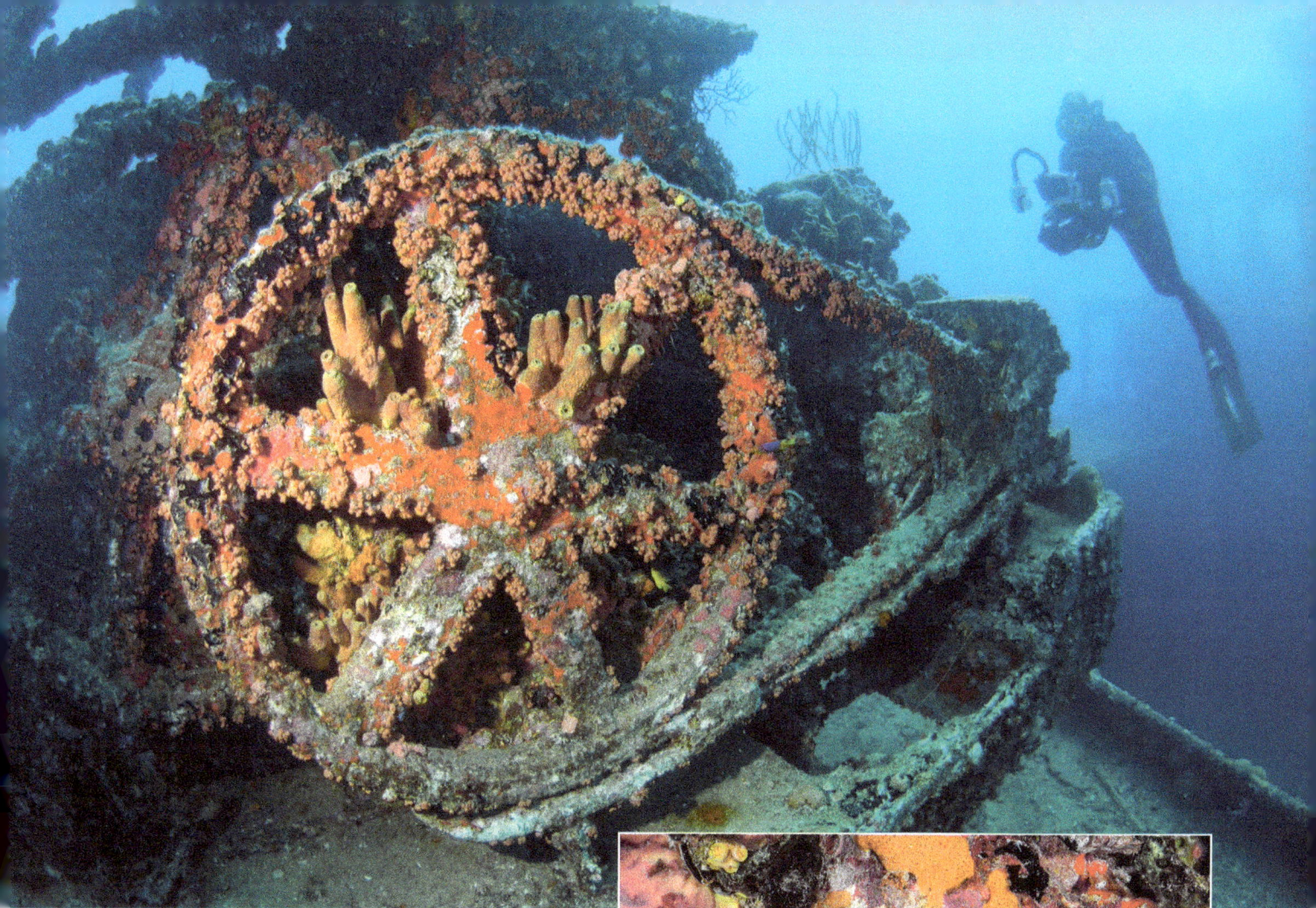

Built in 1942, the USS LST-467 was a U.S. Navy LST-1 class tank landing ship used in the Asia-Pacific theater of operations during World War II.

>>ST THOMAS
PRISONER PLANE

Our attention turned to this new wreck as we tried our DIY investigative skills.

The headlines in the newspapers that morning in April 2006 read "Pilot Recounts Miraculous Crash Landing at Sea." We were in St Thomas to dive the W.I.T. Shoal but this article about a new underwater plane wreck was very distracting! It seems that 4 juvenile detainees and 2 corrections officer were being flown from St. Croix to St Thomas on a Piper Nava-jo owned by the Virgin Islands Department of Justice when the plane's twin engines stopped working. With great skill, the pilot landed the plane on the water without capsizing. The prisoners' handcuffs were removed and everyone escaped into a yellow inflatable raft. Nice ending to a horrible story.

But what about the plane wreck? Our at-tention turned to this new wreck as we tried our DIY investigative skills. Following surface oil spills, plane debris and doing transects while watching our sonar, we were able to lo-cate and dive on this new Virgin Islands' wreck. We looked and didn't touch in order not to in-terfere with the accident scene. As an exercise in shipwreck locating, it was a great success.

NEW PROVIDENCE >>RAY OF HOPE

Everyday, the boats from Stuart Cove's go out, ready to have a close encounter with sharks.
What better location than the Ray of Hope wreck.

In 2003, Nassau port authorities gave the 200-ft freighter, Ray of Hope to Stuart Cove's for sinking as an artificial reef. The ship was sunk in 60 feet of water with the Tongue-of-the-Ocean wall right behind. Ray of Hope was sunk next to an older wreck called Bahama Mama. The hull of the Bahama Mama had begun to deteriorate and only the bow and the stern section still stood upright. But now, these two shipwrecks, side by side, create a spectacular and photogenic site... especially with some sharks wandering past.... and everyone loves sharks!

Well maybe not everyone.... but despite the apprehension surrounded a shark encounter, tourists spend big bucks every year to have an extreme adventure with sharks. Twice a day, everyday, the boats from Stuart Cove's go out, full of tourists ready to have a close encounter with Caribbean reef sharks. And what better location than the Ray of Hope wreck.

Leon Joubert and Claudia Pellarini have been feeding the sharks for years now. Both Leon and Claudia can show you their scars. It's a hazard of the profession and both have had seriously close encounters with sharks and risked losing their limbs and maybe even their lives.

Leon prepared a shark feeding show and we went out to dive on The Ray of Hope, where sharks are regularly fed. Shark feeding is a practice disputed by most ecologists. By feeding sharks, they are disturbed from their normal eating habits and they lose their natural distrust of humans. As they no longer fear divers, they can become aggressive and attack.

The diver in charge of distributing the bait

was dressed in a coat of mail armour over his dive suit. One would think a Roman gladiator. In his box, he had pieces of frozen fish that he distributed at the end of a stick.

The boat headed out to anchor at the edge of the drop-off, where the Caribbean reef sharks live. Sharks hunt in the current in the deep blue and they only come up on the plateau for good reason. The engine stopped and within seconds, they were there: twenty, thirty sharks turning in circles under the hull and cutting the surface with their fins. It's a really impressive sight and we hesitated a few seconds before jumping into the water. But the sharks moved away, watching attentively, and we swam down to the wreck.

The gladiator-cum-diver with his bait box joined us and immediately, the atmosphere changed. As soon as the box was opened and the first bait offered, the sharks rushed in, twisting their bodies and whipping their tails around in a frenzied ball. The shark ballet exploded. Then a single shark rushed out of the ball with a grouper head in its mouth, chased by his slower friends. This madness repeated itself until the last piece of bait was gone. The sharks then calmed down and swam away quietly. They descended along the vertiginous drop-off, into a world far too deep for us.

Dominique swam away from the wreck, looking for the best angle for his painting. Sitting quietly on the sand with his drawing board, he started to sketch. From out in the blue, two sharks came in for a closer look. Dominique held his breath and let them approach. The sharks showed no aggressiveness and it was simple curiosity between sharks and human.

Sharks are very misunderstood creatures. For years, we have been fed stories depicting sharks in a frightening light - the murderous shark, the merciless killer, the wild beast. The newspapers publish articles every time a swimmer or surfer is bitten by a confused shark, while every year we kill millions of sharks.

From this shark feeding dive, we saw how easy it is to create dramatic shark footage. A bit of bait, scary music and some quick editing and one could make these sharks appear as blood thirsty monsters.

In my opinion, by organizing this shark feeding, Stuart is protecting these sharks. Sharks are part of the scuba-biz and as Stuart's associates, these sharks have acquired a recognized value in a market economy. Thousands of tourists come to Stuart Cove's to see sharks and so they have more value alive than dead. It is not really ideal but I prefer to see sharks fed and alive than dead in a soup.

The Ray of Hope is now the 16th wreck sunk on the southwestern side of New Providence.

NEW PROVIDENCE
>>THE WILLAURIE

Where once the inter-island mail was stored is now a spectacular underwater cage, covered by sponges and corals.

The Willaurie was a 130 foot steel freighter built in the Netherlands in 1966. It began its Bahamas career in 1980 as a mailboat, transporting packages between the post office in Nassau and the outer Bahamas islands of Rum Cay, San Sal and Cat Island.

The Willaurie's hull line was clean, European, giving the boat an exotic air. But the hull line was very low, which is suitable for coastal waters but less so for open ocean passages to places like the Southern Bahamas. This flaw would eventually determine its fate.

In the first year of operations in the Bahamas, the boat's ill-fate began. Whilst carrying mail and passengers, the vessel experienced engine trouble and passengers were offloaded aboard a Royal Bahamas Defence Force vessel. Other incidences would follow and in 1988, after being towed in heavy seas, the Willaurie sank at Clifton Pier, becoming an obstacle for boat traffic. The boat's final captain, local dive operator Stuart Cove's, patched the hull and towed the vessel several miles west of New Providence, where the Willaurie's final resting place is.

The hull sunk vertically in 50 feet

of water on a white sand bottom, dotted with coral patches. After more than 30 years under the water, the wreck has become a colourful artificial reef. The most spectacular feature of this wreck is a magnificent cargo compartment, where the letters and the packages were stored. Now, with only the metal support bars left, it is an underwater cage on which sponges and corals have found an ideal place to grow. Fish swim between the bars and leave of their own free will. Dominique decided to play Peter Pan, free-diving between the bars in a game of hide and seek. Ah! With the French, it's always fun!

Next to the wreck of the Willaurie is another wreck. All that is left of this vessel is a destroyed wooden hull, two engines, a propeller shaft and metal debris. We swam out over the sand to get a closer look. Quite dramatic, it is nothing like the Willaurie, a wreck sunk for divers. Where did this boat come from? After some inquiries, it turns out that this boat, loaded with Haitian refugees and exhausted by a long crossing, anchored on this spot the night of its arrival, waiting to land ashore discreetly. Alas, their boat was taking on water and it sank a few hundred meters from the shore, drowning hopes of unfortunate illegal immigrants who wanted to find their place in Nassau's capitalist paradise.

SS Sapona was a concrete-hulled cargo steamer that ran aground near Bimini during a hurricane in 1926.

BIMINI >>THE SS SAPONA

The wreck of the Sapona is easily visible above the water, and is both a navigational landmark for boaters and a popular dive site.

A stay in Bimini is not complete without a bit of freediving both on the Sapona wreck and a site nearby where there is a resident population of Caribbean reef sharks, used to getting close and personal with snorkelers.

The Sapona was built by the Liberty Ship Building Company of Wilmington, North Carolina, as part of a fleet of concrete ships authorized by Woodrow Wilson during World War I because steel was in short supply. Like many others in the fleet, the ship was completed after the end of the war. The Sapona was sold to Carl Fisher, one of the developers of Miami Beach. It was initially used as a casino and later for oil storage. The 1936 book Miami Millions

claims that Mr. Fisher took it out to sea and sank it, but it was in fact purchased in 1924 by Bruce Bethel. Bethel moved the ship to Bimini, using it as a warehouse for alcohol during the era of Prohibition. Bethel also intended to use the ship as a floating nightclub, although this plan never came to fruition. In 1926 the ship ran aground in a hurricane and broke apart.

During World War II, the wreck was used for target practice by the U.S. Army and Navy. The wreck lies in about 15 feet of water, the stern broken off and partially submerged by a hurricane that struck in 2004. Little concrete is left on the hull because of the effects of bombing and weathering.

>>NEW PROVIDENCE
THE VULCAN BOMBER

The wrecks of the Bahamas have kept the memory of 007.

Do you know dear cinephile divers, where the first version of 20,000 Leagues Under the Sea was filmed in 1912? And the first television series of Flipper? What about the underwater scenes of two James Bond films - Thunderball and Never Say Never Again with the real, the only 007, Sean Connery himself, the spy who saves the Western world while seducing beautiful women? I'll give you the answer: these films were shot in Nassau.

Hollywood has produced a long series of films inspired by the underwater world - a disturbing world, populated by giant octopuses, sperm whales, sea snakes and other monstrous creatures out of the delirious imagination of scriptwriters. Most of these films were shot in this corner of the Bahamas at Stuart Coves.

On the walls, photos bear witness to the film shoots, actors and stars of show biz who have come to the Stuart Coves' dive shop.

Stuart discovered the mysterious formula, sought by the alchemists of the Middle Ages, how to make gold from scrap! The formula is simple: mix a rusted freighter with warm, clear sea water, add a few sharks and a shallow coral reef. By sinking wrecks, Stuart was able to create artificial reefs. Stuart convinced the local authorities to give him some old rusted cargo ships that blocked the harbour, in order to transform them into film sets and dive sites.

A structure of tubes covered stands on a sandy bottom. This is the remains of the set which was used to shoot the underwater sequences of the James Bond film Thunderball and the oldest of the Hollywood wrecks. In Thunderball, the ugly Draco, a one-eyed Italian with a blindfold, staged a hell of a plan. With his Spectre buddies, he stole a Vulcan bomber with the nuclear bombs on board. The bomber lands at sea. The evil divers kill the pilot and take the bombs that they will use to blow up the United States. Fortunately James is there to save the situation.

The movie producers created a Vulcan bomber from steel pipe and fiberglass. Today the fiberglass is gone but we can still recognize the shape of the wings, the cabin, the landing gear. The sea has created a superb living lace of gorgonians and sponges which are fixed on the tubes, transforming the sinister bomber into a cathedral. Through the branches, light plays like behind stained glass.

Other famous Hollywood wrecks at Stuart Coves is the 90-foot freighter Tears of Allah used in the Never Say Never Again James Bond movie, a small Cessna 310 wreck which was purposely crashed at sea for the Jaws 3 movie and the treasure wreck from Into The Blue.

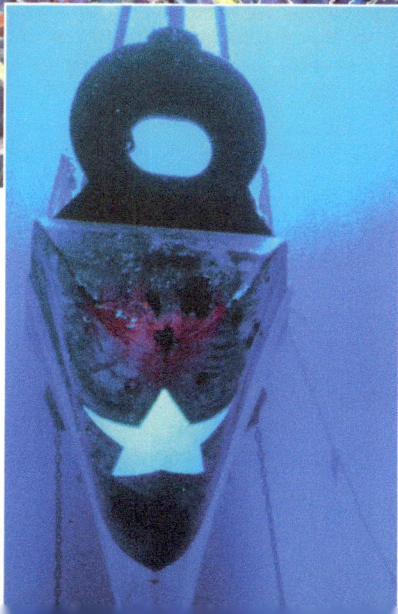

>>CAYMAN BRAC
THE CAPTAIN KEITH TIBBETTS

In September 1996, a Russian military frigate, known
as Destroyer #356, was sunk in Cayman Brac
to make an artificial reef.

113

Wait… how did a Russian frigate get to Cayman Brac? This frigate was first designed and built in 1984 in the Soviet Union during the Cold War era. It crossed the Atlantic to reach Cuban waters in order to defend the communist paradise of Fidel Castro from the aggressions of the American imperialist capitalists. But history has surprises. The Soviet Communist Empire collapsed like a house of cards, the Berlin Wall was destroyed and over-night, millions of citizens who lived under the rules of the Communist system awoke free… free to discover the charms of our liberal society, the market economy, the Russian mafia and the taste of MacDonalds in Red Square.

In Cuba, Fidel Castro weathered the storm. The Castro regime opened its doors to emigrants who fled Florida and to European tour-ists who came to spend their dollars in Cuba and dance the merengue with beautiful Cuban women. And this Russian frigate, rusting away in an arsenal was disarmed and sold to Cayman Brac in the mid-1990s. Towed then cleaned and sunk in 80 feet of water and re-named the M/V Captain Keith Tibbetts, or "the Captain Keith", it has become a very appreciated dive site.

Half an hour after the sinking, Dominique went down with his drawing board to make a sketch of the wreck. The frigate looked good with its guns pointing to the surface and its thin bow marked with the red star. For the occasion of the sinking, Dominique made a painting of the wreck in its new resting place with groupers, barracudas, turtles and angel-fish, who quickly arrived to adopt the wreck as a new home. It is a great memory for Dominique and a beautiful painting.

Skip forward to 2006, 10 years after the ship's sinking. It's ten o'clock in the morning and we have already sailed from Grand Cayman to Cayman Brac and arrived on the spot, directly above the wreck of the Captain Tibbetts. Cathy, Dominique and the DreamWrecks TV team, have returned to the wreck to make an episode about how the 10 years under-water have effected the wreck. Has the coral

This Russian frigate, rusted out in a Cuban arsenal, was disarmed and sold to Cayman Brac in the mid-1990s.

grown on the cannons and the machine guns? Have the instruments of war and death been transformed into an artificial reef as hoped for by those who organized its sinking? To find out, we jump in the water!

A sober silhouette is cut out on the white sand but unfortunately broken in two. In 2004, a hurricane twisted and broke the hull through the mid-section like a toy. The rear of the frigate held up well, but the centre is smashed and folded. The hull is disemboweled and the cables and engine parts are spread-out and intertwined. It's a bit sad to see.

All the passageways which had been closed to entry are now accessible. The metallic barriers have fallen and nothing prevented us from snooping around in the dark recesses of the wreck and accessing the engine room. Sponges have slowly began to cover the wreck and some barracudas and groupers have found a home in its hull. But few other fish have settled in the wreck - they don't seem attracted by the communist propaganda, preferring to swim around on the nearby reef.

Sunk at a shallow depth of 80 feet to be accessible to divers within PADI dive depth limits, the wreck was bound to be tossed around by storms and such will be the fate of this wreck. In 2017 after our last visit, a big storm took off the main section of the stern. Now much of the wreck is a tangled mess.

The wreck, still a spectacular landmark with its set of guns at the bow, is 330 feet in length and lies on its side between 2 coral reefs on Cayman Brac's north shore.

GRAND CAYMAN >> THE CARRIE LEE

Suspended over the edge of an underwater abyss, the Carrie Lee looks like it could, at any moment, slide and plummet into the deep blue. Gone for ever.

We had heard about a notorious offshore shipwreck in the waters of the Cayman Islands, where large congregations of fish and sharks shelter. We flew to Grand Cayman to find it but once on site, as quite often is the case, weather patterns did not comply and the possibility of diving 20 kilometres offshore was next to impossible. Back at the hotel bar, it was happy hour and while drowning our sorrows, we met a seasoned diver called Ivan, who had worked

in the Cayman dive industry for years. To console us, he started to tell us about some other wrecks that he had come across over the years and perhaps one that would interest us called the Carrie Lee, which he said was worth a look if we have the time.

The Carrie Lee, a 185 foot barge, was used to carry supplies between Grand Cayman, Cayman Brac and Little Cayman but it capsized and sank off the coast of Grand Cayman.

Many attempts to recover the vessel failed and finally it sunk. The Carrie Lee landed on the sandy bottom, in 300 feet of water, very close to the edge of a sheer vertical drop-off. This vertical drop-off heads straight down into the dark abyss, bottoming out at 8000 feet. All this sounded quite dramatic and peaked our curiosity.

Carrie Lee is definitely what now days we call a "technical dive". And on Cayman, as is

the case on most islands these days, diving to depths of 200-300 feet require special technical diving certificate, mixed gases, rebreathers, redundant rigs and thousands of dollars worth of diving services. Doing these type of dives on air is now a thing of the past, with most dive operators refusing to provide tanks for such activities, deemed too dangerous, even with enriched air decompression.

But we have been doing 300 feet dives on air for a few decades now, long before it was considered dangerous. Agreed that diving at these depths requires experience, careful planning, and know-how but we know all about that. And now at our age, not only do we do enriched air decompression but we like to switch over to pure oxygen for some time before surfacing.

Ivan is from the same generation of divers as we are and after a few beers, with a knowing wink, he agreed to rent us his boat with all the necessary equipment for us to do this not-so-by-the-books wreck dive.

To be honest, diving on the Carrie Lee was going be a challenge. It's deep, lying on a slope with depths varying from 180 feet to 300 feet depending on whether you visit the top of the stern or the bottom of the bow. And there is usually current both on the surface and on the descent line.

At the site was a surface buoy and a gentle current vibrated the descent line which disappeared into the blue. We began our descent along the line, which is attached to the rear of the wreck. At 100 feet, the top of the aft cabin appeared and the silhouette of the hull was visible and stood out on the white sand bottom. Beyond the wreck, the water was very dark crystalline. Jacks came up in the blue to greet us and escorted us down towards the wreck.

We swam above the wreck towards the bow. Suspended in the blue 50 feet over the wreck, Cathy searched for the best angles for her photography while Dominique traced the

118

silhouette of the wreck. As we arrived over the drop-off, we experienced the sheer precarious beauty of this wreck. Hanging on an angle over the edge of the abyss, the boat looked like at any moment it could slide and plummet into the deep blue. Gone for ever.

We dropped 50 feet down to the bow of the boat to look at the anchor winches and across the storage hulls back towards the aft cabin. Our depth gages moved into the red and our limited minutes passed very quickly. Despite the narcosis, Cathy played with her aperture, shutter speed and strobe angles to get the perfect shot.

On a second dive, Cathy completed her images of the wreck with a dive at the stern of the boat. The aft cabin is richly decorated with sponges, gorgonians, sea whips and black coral. A turtle, accompanied by an angel fish came to see us and grazed on sponges on the sea floor. The vision was complete and we headed back to the light of the surface.

To be able to dive as a couple and to share such an intense and exceptional experience is a real gift. We love these trips into the deep blue. They intoxicate us! For a few minutes we forget all our personal problems and those of the planet too. It's a kind of rebirth that you never get tired of it. We look back with fond memories of our few spectacular dives on the Carrie Lee and will cherish the experience for years to come.

The Carrie Lee is completely intact and rests at a depth of 180ft-280ft off the south west coast of Grand Cayman.

GRAND CAYMAN >>THE DOC POULSON

An underwater photography studio, this small wreck brings great delight to divers with its encrusting coral, sponges and sea fans.

The Doc Poulson is a tailor-made wreck, sunk for the tourist market in 1982 in 60 feet of water. Named for a the doctor who set up the first hyperbaric chamber on Grand Cayman, the Doc Poulson was a Japanese cable laying ship before being turned into an artificial reef.

This 80 foot long wreck is a real underwater photography stu-dio, sitting on a bed of white sand not far from a shallow reef with beautiful blue gin-clear water. Blue and stoplight parrotfish cross the sand to visit the wreck and a school of jacks pass by in the blue. The wreck, and particularly the cable winches on deck are encrusted with colourful sponges, sea fans and coral.

During the filming of the DreamWrecks show, our cameramen, Mike and Warren were thrilled because they could work in peace and film from all possible angles. Dominique decided to scooter / free dive the wreck and Cathy took pictures of Dominique and his underwater antics.

We returned to this wreck in 2018 and to our great joy, the wreck has become an even more prolific substrate for coral, sponges and sea fans, despite the disastrous state that we found many of the west end reefs of Grand Cayman.

GRAND CAYMAN
>>USS KITTIWAKE

This vessel, equipped for underwater research, has finally found its place on a bed of white sand in Grand Cayman.

USS Kittiwake (ASR-13) was a United States Navy Chanticleer-class submarine rescue vessel from 1946 to 1994. The primary mission of the Kittiwake was to rescue sailors from downed submarines. Kittiwake accompanied submarines during sea trials and maneuvers where its crew would monitor dive operations and practice underwater-rescue procedures. Kittiwake was very much a diving vessel.

From stories of the crew, there was great camaraderie and both rewarding and challenging voyages onboard. The ex-crew were fond of her and would say "to know her was to love her."

Many of her stories are still locked away as 'classified' but there are some tales that have come to light. In 1959, The Kittiwake set a world record for the deepest submarine-rescue exercise, taking an officer and four others to a depth of 705 feet. One of Kittiwake's best-known stories came after the space shuttle Challenger disaster in 1986. The Department of Defense and the United States Coast Guard undertook a massive search for the space shuttle's black box. It was the Kittiwake and her crew who eventually recovered the Challenger's

black box from the bottom of the Atlantic Ocean.

After almost 50 years of active surface in the US Navy, the USS Kittiwake was decommissioned from the Navy. After being decommissioned, the Kittiwake would wait quietly for 8 years, before being called to another kind of service. In 2009, the ship was donated to the Cayman Islands for the purpose of being sunk as an artificial reef.

Kittiwake was cleaned and prepared for sinking. This expensive and time-consuming process required cleaning the ship of all environmental contaminants and hazardous materials such as PCBs, asbestos and lead-based paint These substances were commonly used in ships built during World War II so the process of removing all of the paint and wires from the five-deck Kittiwake was a lengthy one. In addition to being made environmentally friendly, Kittiwake was also made more dive-friendly. Large holes were cut in its hull to create simple swim-throughs. Many of its doors, hatches, bulkheads and even some floors were removed in preparation for the sinking.

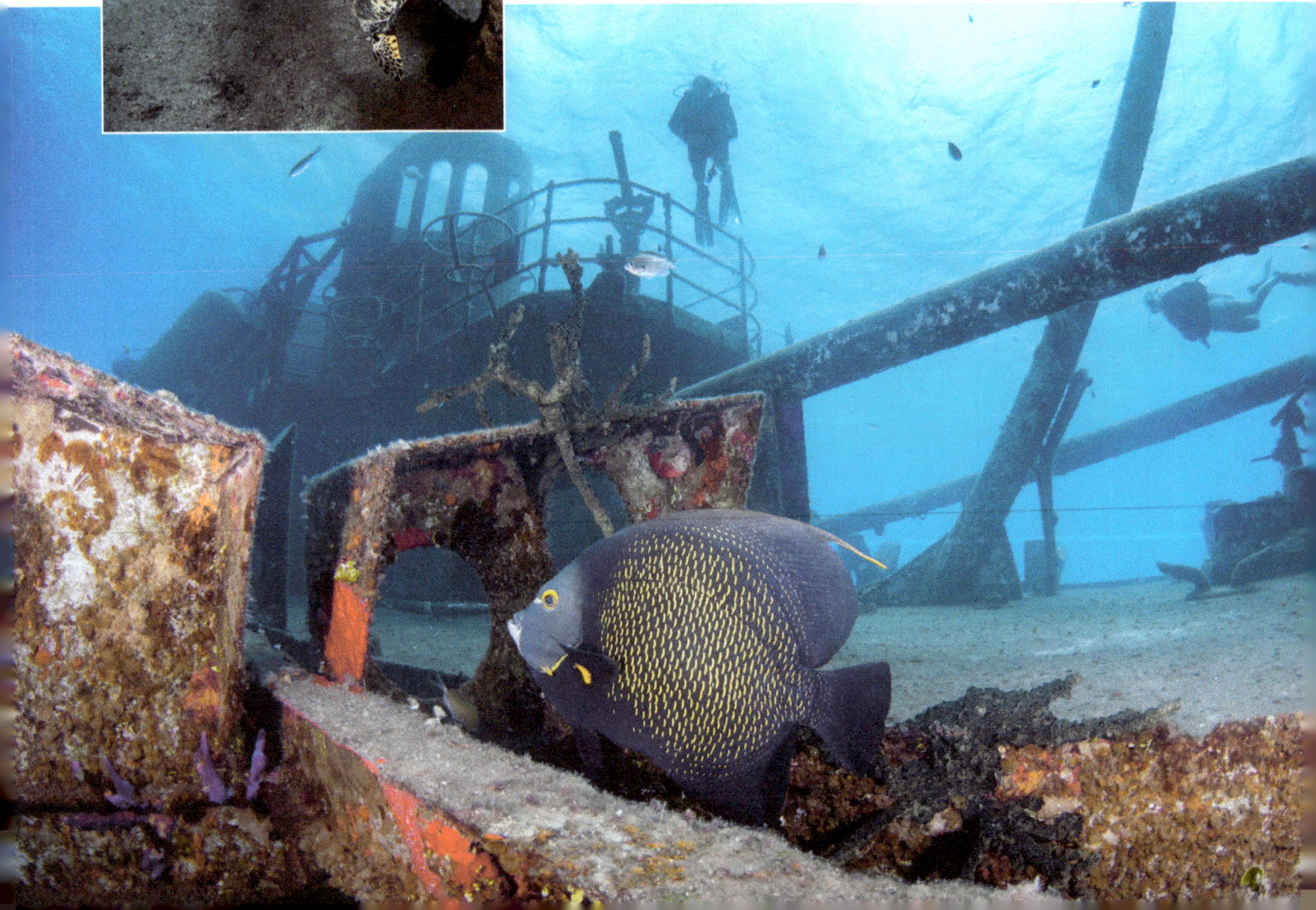

In 2011, the Kittiwake was sunk off Seven Mile Beach in Grand Cayman. The ship was successfully situated underwater in an almost perfectly upright position.

In 2018 on a quick trip to Grand Cayman we had the chance to dive on the Kittiwake. We knew we only had 2 dives on the wreck and so made sure that we were in the water at the crack of dawn, before the hundreds of divers, who dive on the Kittiwake arrived. A second dive around mid-day could capture the dive-mania. I understand why divers flock to this shipwreck. It is definitely impressive! The site of the Kittiwake resting next to the reef in the white Caribbean sand surrounded by crystal clear blue water is truly phenomenal.

The Kittiwake has become home to a diverse range of marine life. All kinds of amazing marine creatures can be found living in the structure like barracuda, schools of horse eyed jacks, turtles, angelfish and groupers. The marine life use both the deck and the inside of the wreck as a large underwater habitat.

On this 250-foot wreck highlights

include the mess hall, the massive propellers and towering smoke stack, two recompression chambers, diving bell, water cannon, giant winches and the deck of the ship full of marine life. The iconic wheel house has been damaged by storms but divers can still pose at the captain's wheel.

In 2017, Tropical Storm Nate snapped Kittiwake's anchor chains and pushed the wreck onto its port side. The Kittiwake sits in 75 feet of water with the shallowest part of the wreck just 27 feet below the surface.

USS Kittiwake (ASR-13) was a Chanticleer-class submarine rescue ship that served in the U.S. Navy from 1946 to 1994.

>>ROATAN
PRINCE ALBERT

The nutrients of the channel have made this wreck a magnet for macro life.

Along the south shore of Roatan lies the wreck of the Prince Albert. The wreck sits upright and intact in 65 feet of water in a sand channel between the lagoon and the outer reef, not far from the mangroves.

Mangroves act as nurseries for juvenile fish and Prince Albert's proximity to them has contributed to the abundant marine life on this wreck. Macro life and juvenile fish are plentiful. We found a pair of seahorses on our first dive on the wreck. Eagle rays, as they hunt for shellfish in the sand channel, pass by the wreck.

The water colour and clarity on the wreck is very variable, dependent on the tides and whether water is going into the lagoon or out. When the tide is going out and the lagoon emptying, the wreck appears to be lost in the fog.

The Prince Albert was the first and perhaps the most successful Ro-

atan wreck intentionally sunk for divers. This island freighter was originally a Nicaraguan cargo ship. Its owner and passengers made safe passage to Honduras and the boat has remained since. In 1985, in a somewhat complicated manoeuvre, including the ship running aground on the reef, the wreck was sunk.

35 years later, the 140' tanker is in remarkably good shape, with most of its structures still intact and significant coral and sponge growth. The wreck has become a virtual magnet for marine life.

ROATAN >>ODYSSEY

In gin-clear water, this ship's massiveness is overwhelming.

The day we dove the Odyssey, the water visibility was other-worldly. It was so clear that if we weren't floating in water, we would have thought we were in outer space. Add to that the lack of fish or any marine creatures and the similarities with the moon's surface were apparent.

A catastrophic fire onboard put an end to the Odyssey's freight-hauling career. Anthony's Key Resort spearheaded the effort to clean, prepare and sink the ship. In 2002, the ship was towed, positioned over its future home, and sunk for the pleasure of divers.

The ship's massiveness is overwhelming - 300 feet from bow to stern, 50 feet wide and 85 feet tall.

With visibility of over 300 foot, we could see the entire vessel which was totally amazing! The cargo area of the Odyssey is the size of a football field. Swimming the length of the hull, we felt dwarfed, like a page out of Alice in Wonderland.

The stern structure leans to starboard giving a strange skewed perspective. Like climbing the Eiffel Tower, we swam up the structure, exploring our way to the bridge. From there we swam forward over the collapsed cargo hold. The bow was upright, providing views of the surrounding reef.

The new home of The Odyssey is off Mud Hole, resting on sand in 110 feet of water.

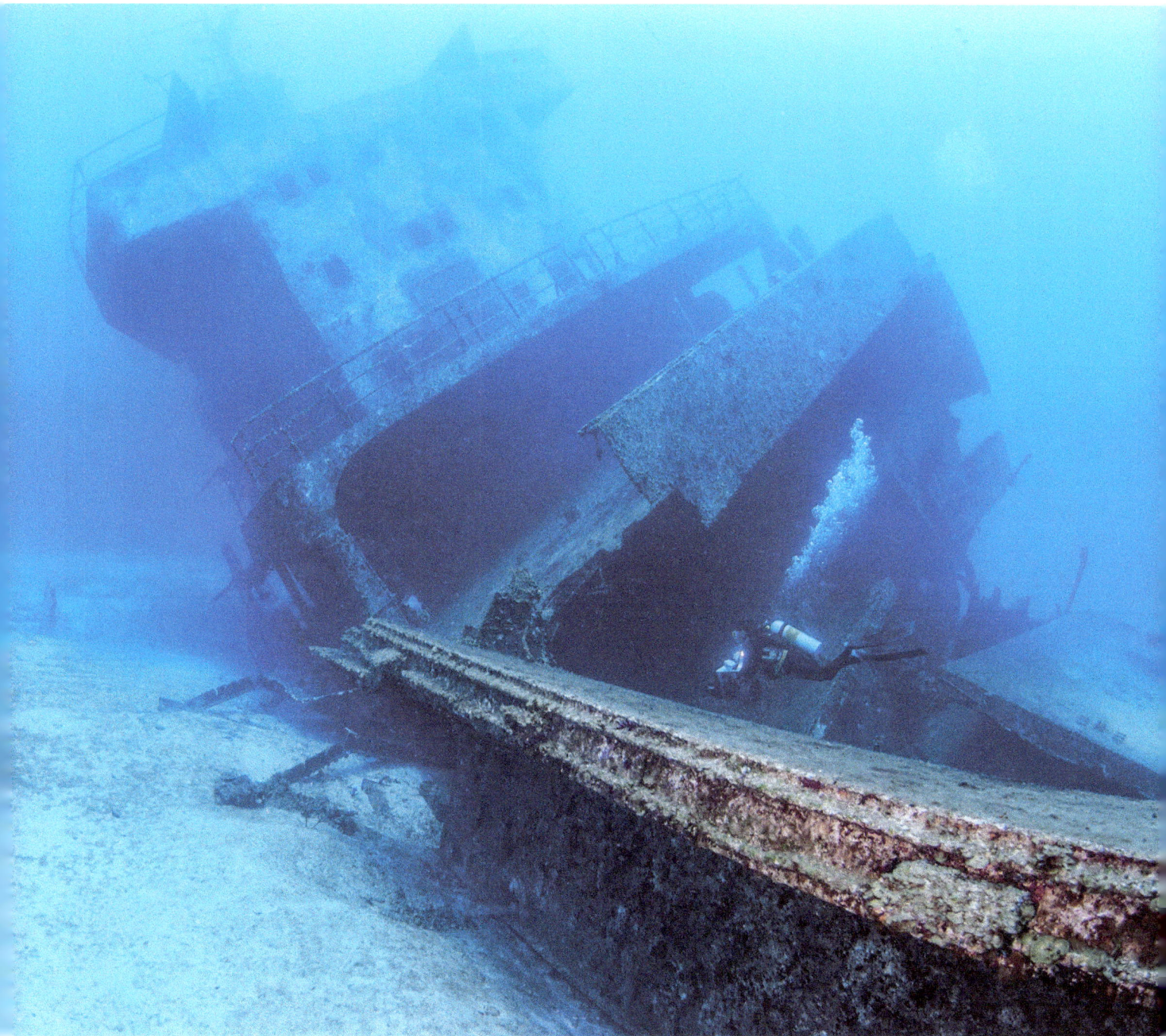

>>ROATAN
EL AGUILA

Broken by a hurricane just one year after it sank, the mangled hull is a great habitat for marine life.

El Aguila is Anthony's Key Resort's house wreck and a short ride away from Sandy Bay. It lies on a bed of sand at 110 feet in depth, not far from the reef. From the reef, the view of the wreck on the sand patch is quite spectacular. The bow is standing upright on its keel and the remains of the mast stand on the deck. Dominique captured this vision on his sketch pad.

The Resort purchased this 230 foot cargo vessel to make a new wreck site for their divers. It took the team 5 weeks between purchasing, cleaning, towing, and finally sinking the ship in its current location. Its final voyage, was a run from Puerto Cortes to Haiti, carrying a cargo of concrete which can be found in the wreckage.

In 1998, one year after El Aguila's sinking, Hurricane Mitch left this wreck in a bit of a mess. Even with the deck 80 feet below the surface it was not safe enough to withstand the full blow of the hurricane. All salvageable metal had been removed from the ship before it sunk, leaving the hull structurally unable to resist the stress created by relentless current and surge. El Aguila split into two with the cargo holds broken lengthwise and separated from the wheelhouse and the bow.

The upside to the destruction of the midsection is that it has provided more habitat for marine species. Now there are plenty of nooks and crannies to explore and on our trips to El Aquila, we swam through the scattered metal debris, where grouper and angelfish have taken refuge.

For the curious, the wheelhouse at the stern of the wreck had numerous passage ways to explore, some with clouds of small bait fish. We had fun playing in this shipwreck-cum-underwater jungle-gym.

PALM BEACH >>ANNA CECILIA

While the summer season in Florida is at its peak, an extraordinary natural event is taking place. This is the spawning period for the goliath grouper. Hundreds gather around wrecks to accomplish a vital mission: to reproduce. The result is one of the most spectacular underwater shows on the planet.

Our adventure began at the West Palm Beach Marina, located on Singer Island. The dive club is called Calypso Divers and we were greeted by our friendly captain, Damien, and his diving guide Guillermo. Stuck at the dock between an armada of fishing boats was our little dive boat - nothing luxurious but everything was in its place and everything worked.

On the way out to our first dive site, Guillermo told us the story of these giant groupers that we were there to see... these groupers who were almost fished to extinction.

Until 1960, goliath groupers were present along the Florida coast. You just had to put your head underwater to see them - hidden in the shade of the pontoons, near the beaches and on the reefs. Due to both their large size and their sedentary nature, spear fishermen wreaked havoc on this easy to harpoon prey.

Able to reach nearly 300 kilos and more than 2.5 metres long, goliath groupers are the largest predatory, reef fish in the Tropical Atlantic and the Caribbean. They have been found on both side of the tropical Atlantic, through the Caribbean and Gulf of Mexico and as far south as Brazil.

But now in most places, these big fish are rare or non-existent. But not so in the waters of Palm Beach County where the law has protected these beautiful creatures. Anytime of the year it is quite common to see at least one or two of these big animals lurking on a wreck or within an undercut on a ledge.

And late into the summer season, a show takes places off the coast of Palm Beach County that divers will not experience anywhere else in the world - congregations of 100 plus mammoth size groupers massed together on a particular handful of wreck sites.

Typically first of August marks the beginning of Goliath Grouper spawning season. And like the fish, it is a goliath event. The area's resident population of goliaths are joined by others from as far as 300 miles away. Some of the spawning fish that end up in Palm Beach County waters begin their journey from considerable distances, and start moving as early as mid July. By August, the bulk of the migrating fish have arrived, swelling the aggregation sites from a handful to a couple of hundreds.

These gatherings are the start of a two-month romance that takes place at a few key sites between Jupiter and Boynton Beach in Palm Beach County. As the seabed is mostly sandy, many scuttled wrecks serve as aggregation sites and shelter during the breeding season. Originally, these wrecks were sunk for local fishermen. They were traps to attract and fix fish, offering fishermen an easy to find fishing post. But these wrecks have also proved to be shelters for the giant groupers. And large, well-preserved wrecks like the Anna Cecilia, seem to be prized by the goliaths.

Seeing an entire spawning aggregation when underwater visibly is good (60-100 feet), is a spectacle that defies words.

The actual mating ritual for goliaths is still somewhat of a mystery. It has been determined that spawning takes place shortly after sunset during a six to seven night period centered on the new moon cycles of August and September. Males mix their sperm with the ovum clouds of females and the fertilized eggs floats with the currents. Most of the eggs are devoured, but a few will give birth to larvae and then goliath babies, which will grow and return in turn to the wrecks of Florida.

In 1994, the goliath grouper was determined to be critically endangered by the International Union of Conservation of Nature (IUCN). Due to relentless and excessive fishing pressure, the goliath species sits on the edge of being wiped out. For generations, fishermen severely depleted goliath stocks, killing immature fish along with the gargantuan adults for food, "hero" photographs and egos.

The tide began to turn for the goliath grouper in 1990 when Florida enacted laws that completely protected them. Since 1993, harvest and possession of a goliath grouper is prohibited off Florida, Alabama, Mississippi, Louisiana and Texas.

Currently, Florida is the only region where

stocks have returned from a state of collapse. This makes Florida's spawning critically important to the survival of the species. It's the only place in the world where goliath groupers are now found in significant numbers. The comeback of this impressive fish demonstrates nature's resilience and shows that we can turn things around.

A 20 minutes boat ride from the West Palm Beach Marina is a series of 4 wrecks, 165 feet apart called the Mizpah wrecks. They all sit in about 90 feet of water on a sand bed and are meant to be done in a single drift dive, which is quite easy when the current is running. The southern most wreck, and the first wreck of the drift dive, is The Anna Cecilia, a 200 foot cargo ship that was sunk for divers in 2016.

As we neared the dive site of the Mizpah wrecks, Damien informed us that the current should be strong and that we all need to stick together. We decided to jump in upstream of the first wreck and drift into it. As we swam in the blue, the Anna Cecila's ghostly silhouette appeared out of obscurity. The ship was impressively: vertical, upright and intact and at the bow we got our first glimpse of the goliath groupers. It was a relatively small group of 20 or 30 groupers, almost stationary at the bow of the boat with their noses facing into the current, glued together with their tails moving just a tad - enough to keep them in place. Some were white, some black, some gray and the largest was more than two meters long. I have never seen goliaths so close. They allowed us to approach and didn't seem to fear our presence. What an impressive site!

We were mesmerized and could have stayed for hours but after ten minutes or so, our group decided to move on to the second of the Mizpah wrecks. The second wreck, called The Mizpah, is a larger wreck. Sunk in 1968 as an artificial reef, this 300 foot vessel is quite broken up. Only a couple of suspicious groupers were on the wreck and they quickly disappeared as soon as we approached. It seems that this older wreck was of less interest to the goliath groupers than the Anna Cecilia. Perhaps now that it is quite flat, it offers less shelter to the fish.

Our first dive on these two wrecks was reassuring as the groupers were gathering. And we were lucky because the diving conditions were good and in Florida that is not always the case. The water was cold but the visibility was really quite good. The plan was to return to the same dive site for the next few days and try our luck again.

Day 2 we returned to the Anna Cecilia. The groupers were still there but in greater numbers than the day before: about fifty of them. Unfortunately the current was much stronger and it hindered our observation and Cathy's photography. To be able to stay close to the groupers at the bow, Cathy had to wrap her legs around the railing of the ship and hold on, riding the wreck like a horse. After 30 minutes in the company of these magnificent creatures, it was time to leave the Anna Cecilia and drift off into the current.

Back on board, the captain explained that the closer we get to the full moon, the stronger the tidal current will be, but the number of groupers will increase as well. "My friends," concludes Damien, "I think you'd better come back tomorrow".

The next day we returned once again to test our lucky stars. The captain agreed to drop us off alone on the Anna Cecilia and to put the other divers on the Mizpah wreck. Good deal! And, indeed, on this third day we hit the mega jackpot!

Alone on the Anna Cecilia, we discovered a group of goliaths so vast, that they seems to stretch to infinity into the blue. There were hundreds of individuals - male and female, dancing together, rubbing and stroking each other with no regard to our presence. A few lay on the sand, in trenches that they had dug, like birds in a nest. While the groupers gave the impression of swimming effortlessly, for us it was an exhausting struggle against the current to move forward towards the head of the group. But you couldn't have asked for better conditions for approaching and observing these giants, in the intimacy of their sex life. It will be a dive that we will remember for the rest of our lives.

BOYNTON BEACH
>>THE CASTOR

Over the past 20 years, the wreck has been broken up by hurricanes. Today, only the stern of the ship is still standing and it is a favorite place for groupers to take refuge.

South of West Palm Beach in a community called Boynton Beach, is another wreck famous for its 20 - 30 resident goliath groupers who live on the wreck all year round. Its called The M/V Castor. During grouper spawning season, The Castor is one of the largest gathering sites and the numbers of goliath groupers on the wreck can jump well above 100.

On our dive boat were two enthusiastic Castor wreck junkies with over 500 dives on the wreck. For the last 5 years, they have been counting and physically measuring the groupers on the wreck. One that they call Wilbur is so accustomed to them that recently it let one of our friends remove a hook that was planted in the corner of his mouth.

A dive on the Castor is a bit of a technical dive. Farther away from the coast than the Anna Cecilia, the wreck is deeper and the current tends to be heavier. We were told that the conditions on the wreck are very

variable and that no two dives on this wreck are the same. You never know what the visibility, current or water temperature is until you are down on the wreck.

Once at the wreck site, a diver jumped in the water with a scooter and fixed a descent line on the wreck. Shortly after, we jumped in and in heavy current, shaking like a flag in the wind, we went down the line to the wreck 110 feet below the surface on the sand.

The M/V Castor was a 240 foot Dutch freighter built in 1970. It was seized in 1999 by the US Coast Guard, carrying 10,000 pounds of cocaine hidden in a shipment of bagged sugar. The crew was arrested and the fate of the seized vessel open for negotiation. In the end, it was sunk in 2001 by the Palm Beach County Artificial Reef Program to concentrate fish for the Floridian fishing community. In the last 20 years, the wreck has been broken up by hurricanes. Now only the stern of the ship, covered by orange cup coral, stands upright and this is the groupers favorite place to seek refuge.

With a group of about 30 goliaths at the stern on the wreck, there isn't much room for many more. The groupers seemed to be vying for the best place, where the current is the strongest. The goliaths allowed us to come along side and we spent precious minutes observing these magnificent creatures.

We decided to make our way towards the bow and we followed the debris laden deck towards the front, fighting the current the whole way. Another gang of groupers was up at the bow, this time surrounded by a cloud of small silvery fish. But helas, our dive time was short as we wanted to make a second dive on the wreck. So we headed back to the stern to join the rest of the divers for our ascent.

Unfortunately, during our surface interval, the weather conditions became too difficult to ensure our safety and recovery so instead of doing a second dive, we returned to the shelter of the coast and the marina.

Back at the marina, we continued to glean information. To date, Florida is the only place in the world where juveniles and adulthood are found in significant numbers. However, if stocks have rebuilt, this fish is not yet completely out of the woods.

The Florida Fish and Wildlife Conservation Commission is studying the possibility of "limited catches" of goliaths, on the pretext (unfounded) that these animals could be responsible for the decrease in fish and lobster stocks. They are proposing that 100 breeding goliaths could be taken each year for four years. However, many scientists concur that the current population would not last more than one, even two years after the opening of this regulated limit fishery.

One thing is clear: the goliath grouper is now an integral part of local underwater tourism. A 2-tank dive outing to see these amazing creatures costs $125. Thus, these groupers generate for an average dive operation, a few hundred thousand dollars annually. The economic stakes are high and the dive shops and divers are struggling for the protection of the goliath grouper. Thank goodness that in this case, ecology rhymes with economy. Long live these marvellous creatures!

DOMINIQUE
SERAFINI

A young student at the Ecole de Beaux-Arts de Paris, I adored the atmosphere of May 1968. I was 22 years old and the whole experience turned my head around. Since that time, where all seemed possible, I have run after my dreams, dreams of liberty, love and art.

One man helped me to actualize my dreams - Jacques Yves Cousteau, a real magician, who brought even the craziest of dreams to life. Like for many terrestrial beings, he opened the doors to the sea and with him I wrote and drew a series of comic books - known in French as bandes-dessinées which told of the adventures of the Cousteau team. A wonderful adventure that lasted 20 years, I was on board the Calypso with the likes of Albert Falco. I learned how to respect the sea, to dive and visit the sea silently and carefully, in admiration of sea creatures.

After the death of commandant Cousteau, I have continued to live my life at large, diving and sailing the seas with my paint brushes, watercolors and canvases. Drawing under the sea is always wonderful. I continue to work defending the sea, with the likes of Paul Watson (Sea Shepherd), Jean-Michel Cousteau (Ocean Futures) and Patrick Deixonne (Expédition 7e Continent). With my drawings, paintings and graphic novels, I share my fascination for the underwater world with children, inciting them to respect and defend it.

www.dominiqueserafini.com
domiserafini@gmail.com
facebook.com/domiserafini

CATHY
SALISBURY

I have been a visual artist all my life. Born and raised in Montreal, I graduated University in 1986 with a Bachelors in Fine Arts in film and photography from Concordia University.

My creative life began by making angst filled art movies and experimental documentaries, that I shared in industrial spaces with extreme musical performances. I then moved to using my creative skills to speak to much larger audiences - on newsprint. I started and published alternative newsweeklies in both Montreal and Halifax. Speaking about music, film and the arts to hundreds of thousands of readers every week and covering what the mainstream press ignored was a passion that I pursued for many years.

With all the weekly newspaper deadlines, I only started scuba diving in my late 20s. But once I put my head under the water, all I wanted to do was discover and explore this wonderful liquid world. Even newspaper conventions were an opportunity to get into the water and explore a new corner of the underwater world.

On New Years Eve 1999, I arrived in Bonaire and immediately knew that the marine world here was something that I could grow old with and care for. Shortly after, I met the legendary frenchman Dominique Serafini, a world acclaimed underwater painter and illustrator, and a member of Jacques Cousteau's team. There were sparks in the air and it was clear that we were meant to be together, to love each other but more importantly to dive together and collaborate on all kinds of creative projects to do with our undersea world.

www.catherinesalisbury.com
cathsalis@gmail.com
facebook.com/cathysalisburysubaqua

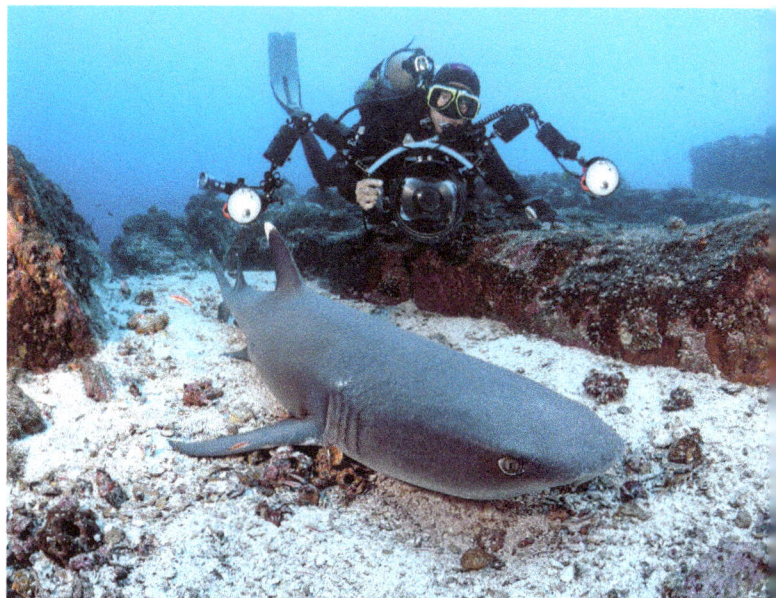

DREAMWRECKS

Dominique and Cathy's first project together was a book about the most spectacular shipwrecks of Aruba, Bonaire and Curacao called DreamWrecks, published in 2001. Cathy bought her first underwater housing in order to take photos for the book.

In 2006, the book was the inspiration for the weekly television show DreamWrecks which Cathy and Dominique hosted. This 26 part tv series had a broader focus - this time the shipwrecks of the Caribbean. The show followed the couple in their adventures. Cathy photographed and Dominique sketched and painted the wrecks, all the while telling the story behind the vessel. The series has aired all around the world.

Their collaborative work does not stop there. Dominique and Cathy have done other joint publication works and they regularly exhibit their paintings and photography.

Through their creative works, they try to show people how magical a place the underwater world is and they hope to inspire others to love it as much as they do.

www.dreamwrecks.com

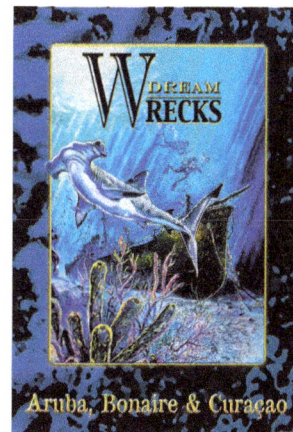

www.ingramcontent.com/pod-product-compliance
Lightning Source LLC
Chambersburg PA
CBHW051556030426

42334CB00034B/3454